Please return/renew this item by the last due date.
Library items may be renewed by phone on
030 33 33 1234 (24 hours) or via our website
www.cumbria.gov.uk/libraries

Cumbria Libraries
CLIC
Interactive Catalogue

Ask for a CLIC password

Sophie

DOG OVERBOARD

The Incredible
True Adventures of
the Castaway Dog

EMMA PEARSE

HODDER

First published in 2011 by Hodder & Stoughton
An Hachette UK company

First published in paperback in 2012

1

Copyright © Emma Pearse 2011

The right of Emma Pearse to be identified as the Author of the
Work has been asserted by her in accordance with the Copyright,
Designs and Patents Act 1988.

A CIP catalogue record for this title is available from the British Library

Hardback ISBN 978 1 444 71519 4
Paperback ISBN 978 1 444 71522 4
eBook ISBN 978 1 444 71521 7

Typeset in Plantin Light by Hewer Text UK Ltd, Edinburgh

Printed and bound by Clays Ltd, St Ives plc

Hodder & Stoughton policy is to use papers that are natural, renewable
and recyclable products and made from wood grown in sustainable forests.
The logging and manufacturing processes are expected to conform to
the environmental regulations of the country of origin.

Hodder & Stoughton Ltd
338 Euston Road
London NW1 3BH

www.hodder.co.uk

For Biggles, Poppy, Harmony, Groo, Molly, Molly, Chloe, Lucy, and Oscar.

For Ruby.

For Sophie.

Contents

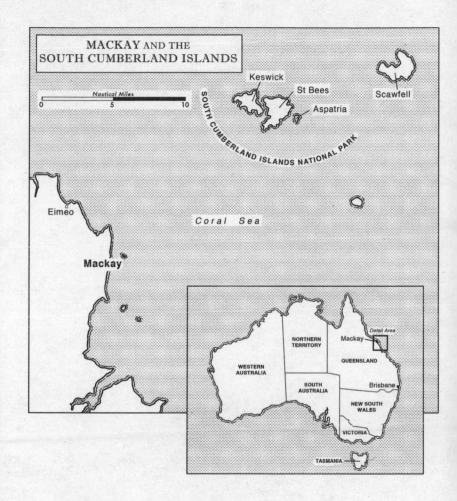

MACKAY AND THE
SOUTH CUMBERLAND ISLANDS

Nautical Miles

0   5   10

Keswick

St Bees

Aspatria

Scawfell

SOUTH CUMBERLAND ISLANDS NATIONAL PARK

Eimeo

Coral   Sea

Mackay

WESTERN
AUSTRALIA

NORTHERN
TERRITORY

Mackay

Detail Area

QUEENSLAND

SOUTH
AUSTRALIA

Brisbane

NEW SOUTH
WALES

VICTORIA

TASMANIA

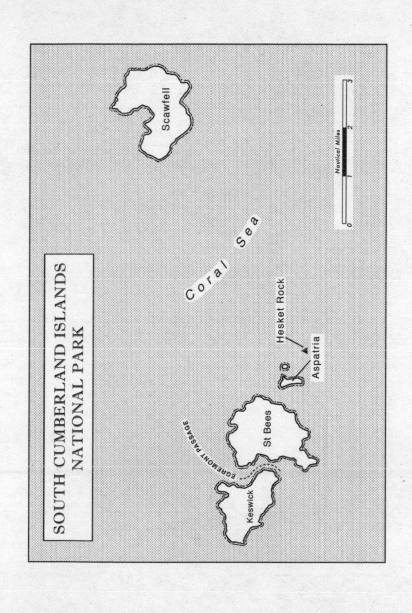

SOUTH CUMBERLAND ISLANDS
NATIONAL PARK

Scawfell

Coral Sea

Hesket Rock

Aspatria

St Bees

EGREMONT PASSAGE

Keswick

Nautical Miles

0   1   2   3

Introduction

Lone Dog in the Wild . . .

It was a warm Sunday evening at the end of March 2009 and the sun was setting over the coral reefs and hundreds of tropical islands dotting Australia's north Queensland coast. On the small island of St Bees, thirty-odd kilometres offshore of Mackay, a small crew of national park rangers and research scientists looked out across the beachfront and saw a dog. Or rather, the silhouette of a dog, a mid-sized wolfish one, trotting along the shoreline. The dog was outlined against the giant orange sun and the darkening ocean, its head hung down and forward, its tail straight out behind.

'There it is,' ranger Steve Burke said to scientist Bill Ellis.

'Lone dog in the wild,' Bill replied.

Bill couldn't help but marvel at the sight. It was like a scene from *The Call of the Wild* out there, the dog gliding through the landscape, seemingly oblivious to the men. It appeared to be determined to keep its distance and follow its solitary path.

Bill, who had been studying the island's koala population since 1998, had just spent the day coaxing koalas out of trees in the island's densely bushy hills. Seeing the running dog on St Bees, though, was an unwelcome novelty. There were wallabies all over the island and there were still plenty of goats, descendents of the animals that were introduced more than a hundred years ago. But by 2009, the approximately 800-hectare island was almost all national park, and protected from both human development and non-native animal species on account of its abundant birdlife, from sacred kingfishers to sea eagles and kites, as well as its occasional snake, and lots of (mostly harmless) spiders.

This dog had no business being on the virtually uninhabited island, in a zone where domestic pets were prohibited. Neither Steve nor Bill was surprised to see it, though. Steve had been aware of the dog for weeks, ever since David Berck, one of the leaseholders of St Bees' only private section, Homestead Bay, called to let him know that there was a dog roaming the island and that it seemed to have come over from Keswick Island, St Bees' neighbour. Some of Keswick's fourteen or so residents had also spotted the dog in December, and then later noticed it on St Bees, which was clearly visible over the narrow but rough ocean channel of Egremont Passage, a few weeks later.

The dog had seemingly been out there for months, yet no one had reported their pet missing. There had been no call to Mackay office of the Queensland Parks and Wildlife Service from distressed dog owners reporting that they had lost their beloved pet whilst out boating. Of course, it had been known to happen: picnicking locals would head out to the islands, their dogs would get lost in the bush and the owners would have to leave them behind in order to catch the tides back to the mainland. But they always alerted the authorities. So for the last few months, Steve and his colleagues had been baffled as to where exactly this dog could have come from and exactly how they should deal with it.

Now, out on St Bees for the first of several annual trips that the Mackay-based rangers made in their supervision of the island, Steve Burke was on a mission. It was time to finally trap this dog. Trapping was the most humane way that he and his fellow rangers, most of them dog lovers with dogs of their own at home, could think of to remove this mysterious animal, who posed a threat to every species on the islands.

But it wasn't going to be easy. The dog had already eluded several attempts by St Bees' sole resident, Peter Berck, to befriend it, tempting it out with cans of dog food. It was giving every impression that it wanted to be left alone, and there were a whole lot of places on St

Bees for it to hide. The island is craggy and volcanic, approximately four kilómetres from shore to shore and shaped like a cartoon egg that has been hastily cracked into a pan. The rangers were only out on the island for four days of solid work and, if they weren't able to lure the dog into the wire trap they'd borrowed from the Mackay Regional Council, Steve knew they were going to have to use more drastic measures. Nobody wanted to take that thought to its conclusion, but the fact was, this dog couldn't be here. If it was behaving antisocially, it could be dangerous. If it was feral, they might have to put it down.

So, the first step was to set the trap in a place the dog was likely to venture to. While there were plenty of spaces to harbour itself, in order to leave St Bees, the creature would have to swim. Steve was counting on it being smart enough to know this, as well as hungry enough to sniff its way into the trap. He and his ranger colleague, Ludi Daucik, hopped into the inflatable dinghy sitting on the shore and headed out to their boat, *Tomoya*. Between them, Steve and Ludi manoeuvred the empty but hefty metal trap from *Tomoya* to the dinghy and then motored back to St Bees. They pulled up beside a rusted line boat that lies on Stockyard Bay, emerging and receding with the tides, looking almost as if it's had a bite taken out of it by one of the hammer-head sharks that live off the reef.

The two men picked a patch under a low-hanging beach-scrub tree above the high tide mark just back from the shore between Honeymoon and Stockyard Bays. It was one of the few sheltered spots visible from Peter's house on Homestead Bay. Steve set about filling a hessian bag with the sloppy contents of several cans of Pal that he'd picked up from the supermarket. He'd bought the fancy beef and gravy recipe, thinking, *this has gotta do the job*. His mind on his kelpie and border collie cross playing safely at home in his Mackay backyard, Steve swished the food around, making sure the gravy seeped into the bag so that the scent would travel further towards this hungry castaway dog's nostrils. He tied the bag to a spring mechanism at the far end of the trap. Any pressure on the hessian bag and the trap would fall down behind the mysterious hound.

After that, there was nothing to be done except to head back to *Tomoya* and get settled for the night. Steve, for one, was looking forward to relaxing in front of the TV, while Bill was ready for a beer.

Bill had been scanning the beach for more evidence of the dog, but there was no sign of it. 'I hope this works,' he said, pointing at the trap now looming in the dusk.

'You and me both, mate,' said Steve.

I

Every Girl Needs a Dog –
Oh Please, Mum . . .

It was the middle of 2005 when Bridget Griffith first set eyes on Sophie. Bridget was a tall, demonstrative sixteen-year-old with almond-shaped eyes and a wicked smile. She was working two holiday jobs at a shopping centre in Mackay, and the object of her affection was a shy, fluffy puppy with her nose pressed into her belly as she lay sleeping behind a window in a pet store. Sophie was the sleepiest of a litter of otherwise bumptious cattle dogs, which in puppydom are white-haired, squashy-nosed and compact, like toy versions of wolves.

Every day during her lunch break, Bridget would go straight to the pet store, which is across the way from the card shop she was working in, and stand in front of the puppies that had no doubt been strategically placed to tantalise every young girl or boy passing by. Bridget would 'Aww' and 'Oh my God' as the male puppies, in particular, wooed her, bouncing and clawing the windows as they looked out at her with their eager eyes. All the while, there was one little puppy that stayed in a furry ball in the corner of the pen, apparently oblivious to the potential suitor tapping at the window, waving and smiling at her.

For years Bridget had been carrying on to her mum and dad about getting a dog. All three of her older siblings had had their own dogs, and Bridget had dreams of a puppy with a super-girly name, like Alicia, who she would take everywhere and have as her companion, much like her brother Luke's dog was to him. Her parents kept saying no. They had one cattle dog already, Luke's Jordy, and in any case, Bridget had commitments all over the place, from basketball to netball and schoolwork, not to mention a popping social life. But it wasn't enough for Bridget. She needed a puppy to share it all with and she was determined to take one of those cattle dogs home.

One dry day in July, Bridget's mother, Jan, a smartly-dressed and dynamic late-fifty-something, drove to the Caneland shopping centre to meet Bridget after work, which was a rare occurrence. Jan had always hated the shopping centre for the same reason she seethed over lots of more recent changes in Mackay – she saw them as the sterilisation of the once idyllic coastal town that had run for decades on the hard work of small-business owners such as herself and Bridget's father, Dave. So this visit to Caneland was to be brief, and Bridget and Jan split up to get everything done as quickly as possible, buying underwear from Best & Less and new basketball uniforms from Lorna Jane.

Bridget decided to make a little detour. She wanted to go see the puppies, even though she knew it would make Jan cranky. But Bridget just had to have a look.

As she walked to the window, she noticed that the litter she'd been eyeing for weeks had been reduced to just two: a boy and a girl. She stood there in front of them, mesmerised more by the boy pup than the girl. The male was mischievously bouncing around, getting its paws entangled in paper, barking at the window and, in general, looking very adoptable, while the female was huddled in a corner, sleeping and seemingly uninterested in even the possibility of attention.

Bridget couldn't help herself; she had to nurse the dogs. She found Jan in Best & Less and begged her to come see the puppies. 'I promise we won't nurse them, I promise,' Bridget lied. Jan was reluctant: she knew that if they cuddled the puppies, that would be that. But it was hard to say no to the vivacious and determined Bridget, who had linked her arm through Jan's and was walking her mother towards the pet store before Jan could stop her.

The minute Jan saw the puppies, her resolve started to melt.

'Can I nurse the boy?' Bridget asked the woman minding the pet store.

'No, nurse the girl,' Jan interjected.

Of the Griffiths' many dogs, all but one had been female. Jan wasn't keen on taking another dog home, but she knew the odds were already stacked against her – at the very least they should stick to the gender they were used to. Dave always believed that female dogs had a better nature than male dogs. 'And besides,' he would say, as if it couldn't be more obvious, 'they don't pee all over everything like males do.'

Bridget picked up the sleepy female puppy, who by this time was shaking. 'She was a really scared little dog,' Bridget remembers. But Bridget held her and stroked her under the chin and calmed her down. The pup was soft and warm, with piles of white-grey fur flecked with blue. She had a slightly upturned nose, like the nose of a little child, and she smelled of dog biscuits and freshly laundered towels. Once calm, the puppy turned her head to Bridget and licked her face. 'Dealbreaker, absolute dealbreaker,' Bridget says now.

Bridget put the puppy back down in the window and mother and daughter walked outside to discuss what getting a new dog was going to mean for the family. Outside, as Bridget worked up every angle to convince her mum that there was no reason not to get a puppy, the tears started to fall. If it took a mini-tantrum, Bridget was prepared to go there. She had been looking at these puppies for weeks, just dying to take one home. She practised the age-old refrain: she would feed it and look after it, she promised. All the other Griffith children had had their own dog, it was her turn now.

Jan wasn't fooled; she knew her theatrical daughter could lay it on thick when she wanted something. Bridget was being over-the-top, but Jan couldn't help sort of admiring her for it. This girl knew what she wanted and how to get it, and in fact, Jan didn't need a whole lot of convincing. She was already smitten with the tiny pups.

Jan agreed to go back into the pet store and let Bridget hold the girl dog once more. Looking on, as Bridget nuzzled with soon-to-be Sophie, Jan clasped her hands over her mouth in adoration. The girl and the puppy looked like they belonged together and clearly they were both falling head over heels. Bridget handed the puppy to her mother and, just like that, another Griffith woman fell hopelessly in love.

Jan told the girl in the store that they were coming back for the female puppy and entreated her not to sell her, but they all knew that the clock was ticking. The rest of the litter had already gone, so there had to be more Bridgets out there trying to convince more Jans that now was the time for that new puppy. Jan just needed to clear it with Dave, who was over at the offices of the family electrical business.

When Jan called to say they needed to talk seriously, Dave became pretty nervous. Dave Griffith was a broad-shouldered man in his early sixties who wasn't generally the nervy type, but it wasn't often that he got a call from his wife of thirty years announcing that they had to have a serious talk. He suddenly worried, *was she going to leave him or something?* He couldn't really believe that there was anything badly amiss, but then again, he had just bought the family's first boat, *Honey May*. She was a 32-foot third-hand motor cruiser with very tight living quarters: two tiny bedrooms and a saloon with faux-leather upholstery. Not exactly a yacht, but still. He'd bought the boat so that he and Jan could enjoy their later years out on the ocean, fishing, whale-watching and relishing the marine paradise that their tropical town afforded them. But when he got the call to say that Jan was on her way over, he began to wonder if this latest toy might have been enough to throw Jan into a bout of wifely discipline.

Dave was mistaken.

Jan pulled up to the office of Dave Griffith Electrical Services and, leaving a highly-excited Bridget in the passenger seat, walked into Dave's office, white pants very crisp and a resolute expression on her lips. 'We're getting a new dog,' she announced.

Dave frowned then raised his eyebrows. Relief flooded through him as he realised that there was no drama after all.

'Yeah, yeah, whatever you want,' he responded to his own relief. 'As long as you're not divorcing me.'

Jan threw her husband a puzzled look as she hurried out of the offices. She was desperate to get back to Caneland.

Bridget, who had climbed out of the passenger seat and was looking over the car, impatiently scanned her mother's face. Jan was smiling and Bridget knew it was a yes. She let out a whoop and jumped back into the car, which sped back to the shopping centre. Bridget was sick with pure tension. If someone had bought the puppy in the meantime, she was just going to die.

Jan parked the car and Bridget ran ahead. There in the window of the store were the two puppies. The girl was sleeping again and the boy was bouncing around, paws pressed to the glass. He probably recognised Bridget by now, for all the time she'd spent fawning over him. As Jan was inside paying for Sophie, Bridget peered once again through the window that had lured her here every day for months. She almost couldn't look at the boy puppy, who was still staring up at her with his tail wagging. Bridget felt terrible about leaving him in there, alone, his little white face turned up to hers. She wasn't going to push her luck, though. After all those years of dreaming about a dog of her own, and all those weeks of visiting the litter of puppies, having just managed to convince her parents that it was time for a new dog, she wasn't going to argue about which pup! Bridget was beside herself with happiness and nothing could dampen her mood. She was going to be the best dog mum ever to Sophie, the very girly name that was the first to come to mind as she walked out to the car with her new best friend.

★　★　★

Bridget and Jan drove through the gate of the family home, a typical 1940s Queenslander with timber panels painted cream and a second, outdoor home of sorts, under the house. The house was a perfect family home, complete with plush bathroom, barbecue area, guest room, and two TV screens – one up, one down – the size of a grown man's boogie board. The upstairs bedrooms – one of them Dave and Jan's, the other a guest room – looked out through mottled latch windows onto a kidney-shaped pool in the front yard, edged with red timber and tropical gardens of hibiscus and royal pines.

When Bridget and Jan pulled in, there was a welcome committee in the form of Jordy, the family dog, who was doing her routine run around the garden before greeting them as they opened the car doors. Bridget swung her legs out of the passenger door and struggled to her feet – her arms were folded around Sophie, whose soggy black nose was nestled in the crook of Bridget's elbow as if she had been born there. Jan noticed that Jordy stopped the welcoming tail-wagging the second she saw Bridget. The old dog's nose didn't take long to stop sniffing, either – she knew that smell. Another dog . . .

The Griffiths are dog people. They've always had dogs; both Jan and Dave grew up with them. Jan's family, who have been in Mackay for four generations, have had various breeds, including an Australian cattle dog named Biddy, who they adopted after someone left her on the passenger seat of Jan's father's car. Dave grew up in one of the many booming surf towns on the central New South Wales coast, before moving north in the 1970s to work as an electrician at the Bowen Basin coal mines. His childhood was spent in the company of a series of dachshunds, every one of them named Tinker. The first Tinker had a harelip; the last one went everywhere with Dave and his younger brother Lloyd, including out on their surfboards, riding the waves with them as they hit the beaches.

Jan and Dave met when Jan was a very attractive bartender at the smoky local bar, Wilkie's, slamming down beers for local tradesmen and mine workers, such as Dave. Their courtship was legendary around Mackay for being both volatile and long: Jan did a lot of telling Dave to 'Pack your bags and get out of here', and Dave did a bunch of promising to change his ways. There were plenty of parties, but the pair also bonded by sharing things with each other that they weren't in the habit of talking about. In his early twenties, Dave had lost his father to a sudden and early death and was still, close to a decade later, very raw over it. Similarly, Jan's family had been hit by tragedy, and Jan was known to demand that people stop talking about her twelve-year-old brother Danny, who had died when she was just thirteen, 'Unless you want me to really lose it'. Neither of them were the type to talk too intensely about their emotions but they found comfort in an unspoken pact between them. Their marriage was a rude awakening to a lot of their friends, who could happily have gone on drinking in Wilkie's, one big happy gang. But the Griffiths were ready for the next stage of life, and it wasn't long before they had two young children, Matthew and Ellen, and a budding family electrical business. Luke and Bridget came along several years later.

Just as Dave and Jan believed that children were best raised with lots of hobbies and activity, as opposed to video games and TV, they also believed that childhood and family life were better with dogs. Matthew had Mack, an unusually docile border collie who was the teacher's pet at puppy obedience school because he was so sweet and well-behaved, unlike Ellen's unofficial pup, Tina, a bossy silky terrier who Ellen took to school in fourth grade posed as Toto, while she was dressed as Dorothy from *The Wizard of Oz*. At one point, the Griffiths had three dogs: Mack, Tina (who ruled the roost) and Biffy, an Australian terrier who Jan and Dave adopted from Jan's parents.

When he was twelve and the family was (temporarily, as it turned out) dog-free, Luke told his mother that he *must* have a cattle dog. His best mate, Adam 'Jenko' Jenkins, a budding working dog enthusiast, had been telling him so, and had just found a litter up for sale. The answer was no: the business had finally kicked into high gear, Bridget was six years old and time-consuming, and Jan and Dave were not ready for another addition to the family. Luke, wide-eyed and well-armed with justifications, said to his mother, 'What sort of a boy grows up without a dog?' Jan couldn't resist her son, or his logic, and along came Jordy, an almost psychotically loyal, blue cattle dog who spent most of her days protecting Luke from anything or anyone who appeared to be making any suspicious moves, which included other members of the family.

Jordy had been around for almost eleven years when Sophie came along, and the aging dog was not happy to find she now had company. When Sophie emerged from the car in Bridget's arms, Jordy growled softly and looked at Bridget, who was preoccupied, rubbing her cheek on Sophie. She took her new pet to the pool area at the front of the house and plopped her on the red timber decking out in the sun. Sophie was drowsy and wobbly and only just managed to shake herself before her hind legs collapsed to one side and she leaned her whole body onto them, her belly flopping in a heap. Bridget got on her knees and crawled around beside her new puppy, nuzzling and rubbing her cheeks all over Sophie's soft white fur. Bridget found one of Jordy's slightly frayed tennis balls and crouched down to roll it at Sophie, who wagged her tail. She didn't know quite what to do with it but gamely clawed at the ball before letting it roll away. Bridget picked Sophie up and let the pup fall back to sleep in her arms.

Had Jordy been younger, she might have made a lot more fuss to ensure that this new dog knew its place, but her fierceness was waning when Sophie became a Griffith. She had heart problems and was suffering from arthritis. And so, as Bridget and Sophie sat by the pool, Jordy retreated to the hole that she'd dug behind a Brazilian cherry shrub in the backyard, into which she often disappeared for a sulk.

Jordy stayed in that hole for most of Sophie's first week, coming out only for meals, which she seemed to have decided were the best moments for her to assert power over the puppy. Jordy would rush to the bowls of food, blocking tiny Sophie, who had no choice but to stand back while Jordy ate. It was a call to order that the puppy seemed to take to without question. She'd sit behind Jordy under the carport, no hackles up and no whining as she watched her superior clean up her bowl, instinctively understanding the pecking order.

Sophie, in fact, didn't seem to question much as a puppy. She spent her first weeks doing very little but sleeping and eating. It got to the point that Bridget began to fret about her. *Why wasn't she more lively, rolling about in the garden and tripping over her tail?* Sophie would sleep in a little basket in the laundry room under the house for hours and hours, only waking to eat, which she did a lot of – her appetite, at least, instilled the family with confidence. Bridget would put bowls of mince and puppy biscuits down in front of her and (so long as Jordy had finished hers) watch Sophie gobble them up in seconds, then promptly flop back for more deep slumber. Bridget learned to stop worrying about her already beloved pet, but she still thought it was a bit freakish. Dave was reassuring, though. 'A puppy's like a baby: all they want to do is sleep and eat.'

It didn't help matters, Luke and Dave thought, that Bridget insisted on carrying Sophie everywhere. Luke was living in a shared house not far from the family home, but he was round there pretty often, and not shy about sharing his opinions on his sister's dog-rearing. Bridget would pick Sophie up like a baby and nurse her for hours, the two of them sitting on the front steps or out by the pool, Sophie curled up, snoring lightly as Bridget flipped through the women's magazines that Jan discarded after doing the crosswords. 'That dog's never going to learn to walk if you don't put her down now and again,' Dave and Luke used to joke. 'At the moment she doesn't even know she's got legs!'

Despite Dave's insistence that everything was fine with the new family member, after a couple of weeks the Griffiths began to wonder whether Sophie might be deaf, which they knew wasn't entirely uncommon in cattle dogs. The young Sophie did not easily pick up on her name. She often didn't turn around or even perk up when Bridget or Jan called out her name over and over, and she sometimes missed out on treats like Schmackos or dinner leftovers because of it.

Sophie's ear, which had flopped endearingly in the pet store, stayed floppy, whereas the ears of most cattle dogs stand up permanently within the first months of life. The floppy ear added to Sophie's cuteness and the Griffiths eventually came to the conclusion that it was probably the result of a sisterly nip from Jordy, the top dog leaving her mark. Nevertheless, it led to a little bit of teasing.

When Ellen, who was living in Brisbane, called to ask how the new puppy was doing, Dave said that Sophie was a lovely dog but a little bit stupid. Jordy, overbearing as she could be, had at least patrolled the house from the moment she became a Griffith, leading her family to believe she might just be the cleverest dog ever. But Sophie seemed to be more concerned with love, affection and daydreaming.

As the enigmatic pup got stronger, though, she started to wander out from her bed to come and join the family. She'd lope over to Bridget, who would be reading by the pool or shooting a few baskets on the family's makeshift basketball court beside the carport, and Bridget would inevitably stop what she was doing to scoop Sophie up for a cuddle, cooing, 'Hello darling girl.' Sophie would lay her chin over Bridget's shoulder and her paws would hang just over Bridget's arm, flopping about as Bridget carried her around.

Bridget used tennis balls to test Sophie's coordination skills, throwing them to the pup, whose jaw was still too narrow to clamp around the ball. It didn't stop her from trying though, and she'd stand ready to receive the slow-flying balls with her mouth open, swaying her whole back half from side to side. But proving her catching skills was the least of Sophie's worries. As her days became more about doing than sleeping, she had an ongoing challenge to contend with in Jordy, who was still the top Griffith dog.

Jordy, built like a nuggety bulldog with a beefy chest,

spent her days surveying the grounds of the Griffiths' home for any ripples in the suburban peace. She would snarl and bark at anyone who came within the vicinity of the family home, and nip at people's heels if they got too close to *her* family. Even Matthew and Dave were victims of Jordy's ankle-biting. Jordy's primary job, as she seemed to understand it, was to protect Luke, and she did this with the ferocity of a midday sunburn.

Her other job, it turned out, once Jordy had made sure that the new arrival knew who was boss, was to guide Sophie in cattle dog ways. The elder dog would take Sophie on her morning, mid-morning, lunchtime, afternoon, mid-afternoon and early evening rounds of the outer edges of the Griffiths' property. She relished her role as Sophie's mentor. The dogs could be lying in the sun, dopey and dreamy, then switch in an instant into stealthy huntresses. Sophie would observe Jordy's demonstration of the most effective way to harass a bird, then follow suit.

Right from those early days, Sophie was an exceptional bird hunter. When the Griffiths stepped out into the backyard they'd find feathers scattered everywhere, mostly the black and white ones of the small but loud peewees, which couldn't stand a chance against their nemesis. From Sophie's sleeping spot in the pool area, out of sight of the backyard, she could come running at the slightest hint of a bird's presence. Once close enough, she'd get down really low and slink towards the unsuspecting bird. Her ears would go back and then she'd pounce, huffing and slobbering, tearing up the ground as she went in for the kill. Sophie could propel herself with those well-fed torso muscles from one end of the Griffiths' yard like a bullet.

Jordy also made sure to let Sophie know her place when it came to bathroom manners. Jordy being top dog, Sophie wasn't allowed to use the lawn as her toilet. Jordy, herself, had always been admirably tidy about her bathroom habits, never leaving unwelcome piles on the lawn, and Sophie was to continue the courtesy. The pup was relegated to the bushes on the garden edges, a habit she has never broken. 'For a long time, I thought she was doing it because she didn't want anyone to watch her,' says Bridget. Sophie would always trot out of sight when she needed to pee. In her six years as a Griffith, Sophie never soiled a carpet or an empty bedroom and, even when she's out with the family, she pads off to a private place to do her business. It might be part modesty, but it must surely also be part obedience: Sophie has never forgotten Jordy's lessons.

The friendly competitiveness between Jordy and Sophie reflected that between Bridget and Luke. The two youngest Griffiths were best buddies and confirmed rivals. Both of them spent much of their childhood without other siblings around everyday and both of them were surprise arrivals for their parents. When Bridget was a cheeky and emotional nine-year-old and Luke a hot-blooded fifteen-year-old, he used to walk past her in the kitchen and say out of the corner of his mouth, 'You were a mistake, you know.'

Eventually Bridget approached her mother to tattle-tale on her older brother's torments. 'He can talk,' Jan apparently responded. As it happens, Bridget and Luke came into the world the same way both Jordy and Sophie came into the Griffith family: unplanned and with undeniable winning power. ('Bridget is the best possible advertisement for having a baby at forty,' Jan has been known to announce.)

As Sophie grew and adapted to her new life with the Griffiths, Jordy's health was going downhill. Her heart was weakening and her arthritis getting worse so, by the time Sophie had been there for a couple of months, the dogs had undergone a role reversal. Jordy now spent most of her days sleeping, barely able to move and without the energy to taunt her new little sister. When Sophie trotted by Jordy in her bed, the top dog wouldn't growl and block Sophie in her path as she had before, challenging her to a game. Jordy might open her eyes and lift her head to watch Sophie pass but she would lay her head back down, leaving Sophie free to continue on her way to the garden or the pool, where Bridget would be working on an assignment or Dave fiddling with mechanics.

Jordy no longer greeted the Griffiths in the carport when they came home; now it was Sophie skipping from one paw to the other in the driveway when they drove through the gate. Jordy wasn't doing her protective rounds of the yard, either, and Jan would look out the kitchen window while she was stirring her grandmother's Maltese Widow's soup over the stove and miss seeing Jordy galloping around the garden perimeter, hackles up, stopping every few seconds to sniff for airborne intruders. Luke came round every afternoon just to sit with his beloved protector under the house. He would entice her out into the backyard and throw a tennis ball up the lawn, but instead of racing at it in pursuit, Jordy would saunter in the general direction of the ball and then flop in the middle of the lawn.

As the days went on, there was a growing sense of dread in the household. They knew Jordy was on her way out. She was suffering and they weren't going to be able to watch it. They had to have her put down, but when the subject came up, the Griffiths had a hard time discussing it. The conversation would veer back to Jordy's prime, with Luke regaling them with stories that they all knew and loved to hear over and over again. The unspoken prospect of what they were going to have to do hung over the Griffith household for weeks. One day, when Jan and Dave had woken to find Jordy more miserable than they'd ever seen her, barely able to move from her bed of blankets as her discomfort elevated, Jan knew she was going to have to face it. Neither Luke nor Dave had been able to volunteer for the job and Jan feared she'd be a basket case if she tried to do it on her own. So she called one of the family's most trusted friends, Luke's best mate from childhood, Jenko, who had put Luke on to Jordy over a decade ago.

'Look, we have a huge favour to ask,' Jan said to Jenko, who was already feeling very taken aback. He knew the Griffiths as second parents and was alarmed to hear the shake in Jan's voice. As Luke's partner in crime, Jenko had spent years of his adolescence with Jordy and was one of the few people who could come through the Griffiths' gate and not have to brace for a nipping. He knew that Jordy was not well but had not realised the direness of the situation.

Jan told Jenko that she'd arranged an appointment with the vet to have Jordy put down. The family hadn't been able to decide on much but that they did not want to prolong their dog's pain. 'She can't go on,' Jan explained. 'She's just not happy anymore. And you can imagine, we're all hopeless. Luke won't do it and Dave is terrible when it comes to death. Would you be prepared to take her to the vet?'

Jenko agreed to do the deed, knowing that Jan wouldn't be asking if the Griffiths didn't really need him. He was attached to Jordy but had also had a lifetime of dealing with the highs and lows of keeping dogs, having been raised with working dogs as pets.

'I felt a little treacherous, taking my best mate's dog to be put down, but we all knew this was the only thing any of us could do to help Jordy,' says Jenko.

While Bridget was at school and Jan and Dave at work, Jenko came to the house and calmly walked the very frail Jordy to the vet's clinic, five hundred metres down the road. It took them half an hour to get there but her last half hour was full of sun and fresh air.

When Dave came home later that afternoon, there was no Jordy sleeping in her bed. He walked up the stairs to the kitchen and said to Jan, 'You've taken her, haven't you?'

Jan nodded and went to Dave, put her hands on his cheeks and gave him a kiss on the lips. He nodded and rubbed her shoulders.

Jan spoke with the vet later that afternoon, who assured her that Jordy had been asleep and beyond pain when she'd gone. 'Do you want the body?' the vet asked her. Jan answered with a categorical no. The Griffiths did not want to bury Jordy in the backyard. She would live on in their memories and stories.

Not for the first time, the Griffiths pulled together to deal with their sadness. Bridget didn't mention Jordy to Jan when she got home from school. She'd been waiting for it to happen any day now. Puppy Sophie had greeted her at the gate and Bridget rolled around with her outside in the garden for comfort. Later, Luke knew immediately that Jordy was gone when he came through the gate for his daily visit. Jordy wasn't in her hole or her bed. Luke bolted up the stairs but stopped before opening the screen door. His eyes were glazed when he stepped inside. 'She's gone, isn't she?' he said to Jan, who nodded, just as she had with

Dave. Luke let out a big sigh. It would be several days before he came to visit again.

Jan and Dave, who had a lot of practice in helping each other cope with grief, tried to be stoical. They had always loved their dogs, but they were not sentimental. A dog was part of the family, but owning pets meant that you had to cope with their loss. Jordy had enjoyed a long and vigorous life and given the whole family a lot of hilarious and joyful moments, but as Dave says, 'What were we going to do? Dig a hole in the garden so that everyone could stand around crying? It's too hard. She was an old dog and she was in pain and we couldn't let her carry on. It was time to let her go.'

Sophie also immediately noticed that Jordy had gone. Over several days, she searched for her old mentor, sniffing tentatively around Jordy's backyard hole and looking questioningly up at Bridget and Jan when they came through the gate. Owners and dog comforted each other. The whole family were grateful that they had Sophie to lavish their attention and affection on, and in fact, the still gangly pup very quickly benefitted from her sister's passing. She was the perfect distraction from the family's sadness and she wasn't going to protest.

It took less than a week for Sophie's energy levels to rise. She was being smothered with love from everyone, including Luke, and so she came to not only accept, but relish her change in status. Now, when Dave or Bridget got the garden hose out, Sophie behaved like the top dog she was in the house. She began to show her true athletic ability. She also became quite the entertainer. As Dave or Bridget unwound the hose, Sophie would start wiggling her behind madly and sniffing along the ground towards the water as if she were creeping up on an unsuspecting cockroach. When Dave raised the hose, the pup would bound over, jumping in and away from the water and snapping at it wildly as if she were playing 'you can't catch me' with a wily snake. The game was just as addictive for the family as it was for Sophie, and when any of the other kids were home, they'd stand around happily watching and commenting as Sophie snapped away at the water, Dave whipping the hose around for more time than might have been strictly necessary.

The Griffiths realised that Sophie, unlike Jordy, was a sucker for water. In Jordy's prime, Dave only had to grab the hose and Jordy was out of there. Jan would look out the kitchen window and spot her, curled in the hole behind the Brazilian cherry with her head resting over the edge. She could stay there for hours, even long after Dave had put the hose away. Anything to avoid the water.

But Sophie promised to be a water dog right from her early days. Even at two months old, she took to the hose with no prompting and provided hours of pride-provoking entertainment for the Griffiths. Her fascination with snapping at the stream, while an endearing enthusiasm, didn't quite extend to the swimming pool, though. Luke never tried to throw Sophie in, the way he had with Jordy, but she would always be anxious when the family was in the pool. She'd run around the red decking, occasionally barking, watching every move. She could camp by the edge of the pool for hours, standing then sitting then lying, while Bridget and her friends mucked around in there. They'd throw her the tennis ball or splash her, or Bridget would swim to the edge for a kiss and Sophie would put her nose to Bridget's and lick her gently. All the while, Sophie would quietly guard. She appeared to have one eye on the action at all times. Bridget felt as though her cuddly pup was ready to jump in at the first sign of any trouble. Her whole attitude expressed, *hey, be careful in there.*

As her personality emerged, Sophie's tenderness won the Griffiths over. Gradually their suspicion that the newest addition to the family was less than intelligent gave way to an admiration for this creature who had poise and self-confidence and didn't feel the need to insist upon attention. She would never nip at anyone's heels or jump without warning on to someone's lap if nobody was talking to her while they ate dinner. She'd never bark in desperation when she wanted to play a game or be picked up and yet she was always up for a snuggle. While Jordy had always been on alert, ready to snap if someone got too close when she wasn't prepared, or barking even if she'd met the visitor walking into the driveway hundreds of times before, Sophie would always submit herself when her friends or family summoned her over to give her love. When the family sat around the dinner table or visitors gathered around the pool, she'd trot over with her head down a little and place her nose on someone's knee. She would sit like a kangaroo, her back legs bent at right angles and splayed outwards so that her whole bottom flattened on the ground.

Although she would regard strangers with caution for an initial period, she was always more concerned with hugs and pats and company than with showing her working-dog brawn. She was at once more placid and more stubborn than most cattle dogs, who are bred to respect their master as well as to work independently.

People talk about people or animals with old souls: the family believes Sophie is an old soul. She seems to come from a different era, one when women wore gloves and learned about etiquette and dogs knew how to maintain their own dignity.

2

The Special One –
Sophie Chooses Her Bestie

Sophie's elegance just made Bridget want to show her new charge off even more. Every Tuesday night, she would take Sophie to puppy preschool and then to basketball. Bridget played at both city and state level, and Sophie attended most of her games. Bridget's coach would roll her eyes in mock exasperation, but every now and then Bridget would take a sneaky look over and see the coach cooing at and patting Sophie. The pup's place was on a bench beside the court where she would sit calmly and watch the game. She'd turn her head from side to side to follow the ball, or Bridget, up and down the court. Sometimes she'd trot back and forth along the bench as the action became louder. When Bridget had time off the court for the team huddle, her face sweaty and head still in the game, Sophie wouldn't race over for attention. She'd lie on her bench, her eyes moving around the room, and sometimes lift her head to look over at the sidelined players, but ultimately give Bridget her space.

During the day, when Bridget had errands to run in one of her parents' cars, Sophie would jump into the front seat of Dave's red Honda or Jan's silver Nissan to accompany Bridget. Sometimes they'd sneak off, partners in crime, to go to the beach for a vigorous game of tennis ball, Sophie having learnt the joys of fetch after her initial fumbling attempts before she was strong enough to actually clench the ball in her jaw. Bridget and Sophie would run into the ocean, the girl diving under waves and the dog swimming out and then back in, her head above the water and mouth pressed firmly shut, determination and deep pleasure in her eyes. As Sophie grew to maturity and gained in confidence, these beach trips became one of her favourite activities. Sophie was not just a willing but an eager swimmer, and would rush into the water on her own after a game of ball, like an athlete washing off after a hard dose of training.

On the way home, Bridget might zip into a shop's car park, put the windows down and leave Sophie standing up and sticking her head out the window, surveying the scene while Bridget picked up the dry-cleaning or some last-minute things that Jan needed to cook dinner. When the pup saw Bridget returning, she'd stand to attention, tail wagging, hips swishing.

'She'd jump into the driver's seat as if to say, "Welcome back. Where we going now?",' recalls Bridget.

Unlike Jordy, who had spent many hours driving around town with Luke in his metallic green 1971 Volkswagen Beetle, growling at anyone but the family who came near the car, Sophie wouldn't grumble or hiss at Bridget's friends. There wasn't an aggressive bone in Sophie's body, but that didn't mean she was a pushover. 'She would never bite anyone but you always knew that she would protect you,' says Bridget. From early on, Sophie had a gentle authority. She did not threaten by growling or nipping, but when they were out and about, or at home with visitors, she always stood close to Bridget, and usually between her and whoever else was around. Her head would drop low and she'd look ahead, her eyes almost sleepy, but one move from the visitors and she'd fix her attention on them. It was more a vibe than an action. 'Her first instinct was always to be kind and friendly,' says Bridget.

Sophie was also sociable and a bit of a flirt, inclined to linger when people stopped to admire her on her walks around the neighbourhood with Bridget. 'It would take an extra fifteen or twenty minutes to do the same walk I used to do with Jordy, because she would want to stop and wag her tail at everyone walking past.'

Her combination of composure and charming giddiness earned Sophie a nickname that slowly and naturally took hold. 'Sophie Tucker' emerged partly in homage to Sophie's vaudevillian namesake, but even more fundamentally because, in the great Aussie tradition, nicknames are rife throughout the Griffith family. It was no surprise that Sophie, too, began to acquire variations on her given name. Jan never knew Dave's real name for the first few months into their courtship – he was simply Griff or Griffo. Luke rarely answers to his own name, as for most of his life he's been called anything but: Lukey, Spooky, G-riff. Jan is Janny, Ellen is Nell and Bridget responds to several, Gitte being Jan's pet name for her, after Brigitte. Matthew is the only one with the obvious – Matty.

So Sophie became Tuck, Sophie Tucker, Soph. When Sophie was galloping along the beach, Bridget would call out, 'Sophie Tucker!' which somehow expressed her delight in her pet's character more fully than just 'Sophie!' And Dave and Luke became especially fond of Tuck and Tucker. 'Tuck' gave her street cred. Like her namesake, she was a lady with attitude. The nickname seemed to encompass all elements of her increasingly infectious disposition. Sophie spoke for her poise, Tucker her boyish energy, and the combination said it all.

When Bridget had her friends over, Sophie was always welcome. There were lots of after-school, spontaneous hangout sessions and then there were parties – meticulously planned costume affairs that usually took place in the barbeque area under the house and centred around the pool. The Griffith home was always the go-to party house, which was the way Dave and Jan liked it, so they could keep an eye on things.

As Bridget and her girlfriends lounged in bikinis or decadent headwear in honour of the latest fancy dress theme, and her mates in board shorts told louder and louder stories, Sophie would often don a party hat and sit on Bridget's lap looking gorgeous. Bridget's friends couldn't help but adore her, and the youngest Griffith didn't have to look far for affirmation that her bias towards her own pet was legitimate. The two of them would bask in the glory of being the centre of attention. They were a super cute double-act and they knew it.

Despite Sophie's conversion into a dedicated sea-swimmer, she never got over her mistrust of the pool. If people were swimming, Sophie would always be up for a game, but she spent most of her time running as if on tiptoe around the edge of the pool, panting and smiling, occasionally barking when someone dived in or showed any sign of throwing her the tennis ball. If Luke was over, he would lure Sophie onto the top step, assuring her that this was just like the water that she swam in at the beach. She'd step down, ears back but with the tip of her tail wagging, and she'd sit there, legs and bottom submerged in water, while Luke played water bombs with his hands, splashing her affectionately as she licked at the spray. Occasionally she'd allow Bridget to pull her in for a quick lap, but ultimately, she preferred being on the sidelines waiting for a game of tennis ball. While she loved the ocean, she seemed, like many dogs, to be spooked by the enclosed water of a swimming pool.

Sophie had her favourites among Bridget's friends. She especially liked one friend, who used to pretty much ignore Sophie even as she sat beside him. He was the kind of guy who didn't say much but when he did speak, everyone listened. Sophie would sit by his side, unfazed that she was getting no attention, sensing a bit of a kindred spirit. To make sure she wasn't missing out on any cuddles that might be going around, though, she would visit Bridget and her other favourite mates, putting her head through people's legs and wagging her tail in anticipation of a friendly pat.

But not everyone got the same treatment. Sophie could be quite selective about who she showered with her affections, and seemed to intuit misbehaviour. There were times when she might have looked as though she weren't paying much attention, lying with her head between her paws as the fun went on around her, but she would always make her presence felt when the energy amped up in ways that didn't please her. If one of Bridget's friends was making a major nuisance of themselves, wobbling when they stood up and getting mouthy, Sophie would sense it. She would go over to the person and sit between them and the rest of the crowd. Usually, it would be someone who Bridget, herself, thought was getting a little out of control. 'It was as if Sophie was issuing a gentle warning, saying, "Calm down, because if not, I might have to teach you a lesson",' Bridget says.

In just three months since her arrival, Sophie had made herself a crucial part of Griffith family life and had won the adoration of pretty much everyone she met. Jordy would never be forgotten, but her successor was turning out to be even more special than Bridget and Jan had realised when they fell in love with her in the pet store. Bridget, especially, was devoted to her dog. In fact, the bond between hound and teen heralded a new era in the Griffith family's relationship with dogs. Until then, both Jan and Dave adhered to a philosophy the illustrious dog whisperer, Cesar Millan, would be proud of: dogs are dogs and people are people. And this applied particularly to cattle dogs. They were bred to work on farms, rounding up cattle and sheep all day in the harsh sun. Dave's standard take on the matter had always been that if Jordy were on a farm, 'she'd be tied to the water tank and thrown a kangaroo leg twice a week for a feed.' In other words, treat dogs like dogs; and dogs, especially working dogs, belong outside.

But Bridget and Sophie had their ways of getting round this, right from the get-go, and Bridget used to sneak Sophie inside and sit the dog on her lap while she watched reruns of *Sex and the City*. Bridget's logic was impeccable: Sophie wasn't sitting on the couch, she was sitting on Bridget! Jan and Dave were also aware that when it came to bedtime, instead of putting Sophie outside as she was supposed to, Bridget would tiptoe past their bedroom with Sophie in her arms and the two would fall asleep together, Sophie at the end of Bridget's bed, keeping her toes cosy. Jan and Dave had a hard time protesting against the pair's obvious delight in each other's company, but their behaviour certainly raised a few eyebrows amongst the older siblings.

Ellen observed that the Griffith family's attitudes had changed since Sophie had arrived. When she came for a visit from Brisbane, she noticed all sorts of old rules being broken. 'I was constantly amazed at how far Bridget and Sophie were pushing things,' she says. 'There was the fact that Bridget would nurse her like a baby, and that Sophie gradually worked her way from the door step, to inside the door, to the living room . . . Jordy used to get in trouble for even sitting on the door step.'

In their downtime, when Bridget wasn't whizzing from basketball to birthday parties, the pair of them would sit for hours on the front steps. It was Bridget's favourite place to sit and think, or not think. Sophie always joined her, lying at Bridget's feet or tucked up beside her, the two of them looking down the steps as the sun shone into the side yard, Bridget considering her future and Sophie just living in the present, relishing the company.

Not everyone was such a complete pushover though. When Luke was back for a few days, and if Bridget was not around, Sophie got a taste of the Luke Griffith school of dog care. The second youngest Griffith stayed downstairs in the theatre room – from there he would plan his raids on Sophie's increasingly privileged position upstairs.

'I'd try to rattle her up to see if she had any mongrel in her,' he says. 'And she did, she got all dingo.' Sophie would run around as Luke chased her. She'd get slinky, body low to the ground, and sneak around the cars parked in the carport. Then the pair would spend hours with Luke throwing the ball for her and Sophie retrieving it as the stars came out. Luke would steal a can of Dave's Fosters from the fridge and have a nightcap before bed. He would often drift off to sleep in the driveway, patting Sophie. 'I'd wake up to her licking my face, reminding me to go to bed.'

The truth was that not even Luke, Jordy's biggest fan, was immune to Sophie's charms. 'She's a bit of a top dog, she's got attitude,' Luke says of Sophie, remembering times at the beach when she was too busy chasing other dogs to heed his first few calls.

Luke took Sophie with him on his first date with his girlfriend, Heather. Luke was keen that Sophie came along with them to the beach. 'I thought it would be good to have her there, just in case I needed an out,' he admits, recalling that he figured he could always pretend that his dog was out of control and needed to be removed from the scene. But Sophie's services as a distraction were not required, which was good, because she behaved perfectly delightfully. She chased a few other dogs and waded in to the shallow waves for a dip, as always, but ultimately she charmed Heather as much as Luke did.

While Luke softened to Sophie's many charms, he still has a tougher analysis of Sophie's personality than does his younger sister. He can't deny his admiration for her grace and enthusiasm, her loyalty and charm, but also says that Sophie has always known how to play on her appeal. 'She's one of those dogs that puffs her chest up a little bit.'

Underneath this is a brotherly gripe that Sophie – like Bridget – has ended up getting a softer version of parental treatment. Bridget is the youngest by far, and by her time, the family business was humming along and Dave was home more often, even in the afternoons, when Bridget came home from school. Luke would say – with sly affection – that Sophie and Bridget are both as bad each other: bright, precious and able to manipulate their way into any situation and anyone's heart. 'Sophie is a bit like Bridget; she knows how to cast her spell,' Luke says. 'I think she plays the game, she knows how everyone is and how to respond to them. She's intuitive.'

On the flip side, Bridget admits that she didn't like Jordy very much. But when she describes Sophie, it's with the parental coo of a mother proud of her awe-inspiring offspring.

Despite Bridget's adoration of Sophie, the romance was destined to have its limits. Sophie arrived in Bridget's life just as Bridget was gearing up for a new phase: her final high school year before university. She was just sixteen when she pleaded with Jan for a dog, and she was desperate for it to happen, partly because it really was her last chance. Bridget would be heading off to uni in just over a year. And in the meantime, she had a lot of things to do, some of which were going to take her away from home.

Just a few short months after Sophie became a Griffith, Bridget left for Germany on a one month cultural exchange. She was torn, though: 'I nearly decided to stay because a month is a long time to miss out on when they're puppies,' she recalls, sounding like a new mother deciding between being a stay-at-home mum and going back to her career.

But go she did, and sure enough, within a month, a lot happened. Bridget got food poisoning and spent days heaving on her host family's bathroom floor, struggling with sickness and her own non-existent Deutsch. Meanwhile, Sophie continued to fill out. She no longer wobbled when she walked, her fur darkened and her head widened, seemingly in a matter of days. While Bridget was experiencing a whole life (and not an easy one, at that) abroad, Sophie was becoming a gleaming animal worthy of a Pal commercial.

Crucially, she also became Dave's dog. Cattle dogs, like teenage girls, need to have a bestie. Without Bridget around to drive through town with or flop under a chair by the pool next to, Sophie needed someone else to follow around the house, and Dave, who wasn't happy without a pool filter to fix or a mission to the shops to fulfil, was the ideal candidate.

Bridget knew things had changed the moment she got home. 'I came back hoping that I'd still be her favourite and I totally wasn't. While I'd been in Germany, she'd become Dad's dog,' says Bridget. She saw she'd become second choice whenever Sophie had an option to stick with Dave. Dave could be sitting under the house with a newspaper and Bridget ready to go for a run and Sophie would stand looking back and forth between them, torn. 'She still loved me but I could tell I had lost her.'

Sophie bonded intently with the man of the house. As inevitably seemed to happen with all the family dogs, Dave slowly emerged as Sophie's prime carer. Sophie seemed to decide that he was the answer to Bridget's absence. It wasn't a calculated thing, it was more that Dave just had an effect on dogs. He would talk to them and they would love to hang out with him as he got busy in the garden or pottered around the pool. Jan's explanation is simple: 'I don't do things that dogs love to do; Dave does.' Dave is a busy guy, a doer who doesn't like to sit still for very long, and he understands that dogs are the same. It's Dave who insists on the family dogs being walked every day, and if it looks like it's not going to happen because of torrential rain, he will become almost as edgy as Sophie. 'The dogs can't be happy, they need their walk,' he'll mutter.

While Bridget was away, Dave fed and chatted to Sophie. It was a crucial time in her life, as she went from sleepy puppy to confident dog. He threw her tennis balls across the swimming pool that she'd catch in her mouth, drop in the water, then nudge across for

Dave to fetch out. He whipped the garden hose around so that Sophie could chase it, snapping her jaws for what seemed like hours in an attempt to catch the water. He took her in the car down to the butcher just as Bridget had and she sat in the passenger seat, ears pricked, looking back and forth between the road ahead and Dave. And the two of them went on endless weekend trips to the beach. Sophie was a dog who really loved the sea. Bridget had reported this to the rest of the family but now Dave saw it for himself. Sophie would stand up in the back seat of the car and rush to put her head out of the window as they arrived at the coast. She seemed to be trying to inhale the sea air, sniffing and barking, her face a pure picture of joy. Once Dave let her off the lead away from people, she'd be off, heading straight for the water.

After Germany, Bridget and Sophie were still good buddies. Sophie would still bound towards Bridget as she came through the front gate in the red Honda, and sit on the bench loyally as Bridget scored points for her basketball team. But when Bridget returned, a few kilos skinnier and full of energy to exert on her cherished pup, Sophie wasn't the desperate, attention-starved pet Bridget sort of hoped for. She had been fed from another hand and seemed to know that, long-term, it was Dave, not Bridget, who was going to drop her pieces of steak or fish from the barbecue as she sat beside him devotedly. It was as if Sophie had figured out that Bridget would come and go, but Dave was there for the long haul.

Sophie now had not one but two of her beloveds wrestling for her attention. Perhaps Sophie knew what she was doing: doubling up on love, as Dave and Bridget quietly vied for the status of favourite.

The two of them would take her down to one of Mackay's quieter beaches and training would be on for daughter and pup. Dave would hold Sophie, her legs twitching as she tried to wriggle free, while Bridget sprinted up the beach. Sophie would whimper and twist and let out a few high-pitched barks before Dave would let her go. From one bestie to another she'd run, tongue out, galloping, gleeful and fast. She'd catch up to Bridget and run around in front of her, forcing Bridget to skid to a stop. Sophie made it clear that she knew the game, and in fact, she was one step ahead. The dog seemed to be herding Bridget the way she would have done cattle or sheep on a farm. There was none of the nipping or biting of ankles that cattle dogs are bred to use to chastise their charges, though. Sophie was in her element and made sure to share it with her family. She'd look back and forth to Dave and Bridget as they took mini breaks mid-game, as if to say, *isn't this amazing?* her tail whipping with joy. Father and daughter egged her on in pure admiration. 'Go, Tuck,' Dave would call out as he released Sophie from his hold. And Bridget would run down to the shore with Sophie following her into the water for a cool-off.

Then the game would start again. Bridget would tell the dog to 'stay,' and Sophie'd look at Dave, breathing heavily, as if to say, *I have to wait?* Dave would hold her as Bridget sprinted back down the beach. Sophie would be twitching, waiting for either one of them to give her the go-ahead. 'Sophie come,' Bridget would say, and Sophie would take off like a child at a school athletics carnival.

But try as Bridget might to win back her bestie, she knew the score. Even when Sophie was on board for an outing with Bridget in the car, she would stop before hopping into the passenger seat and look back at Dave coming down the steps, waiting for him to hop in the car with them. She'd look back and forth between Bridget and Dave tentatively, and Bridget would snap her fingers to lure Sophie in the car. 'I was like, *whoa, did the last six months mean nothing to you?*' Bridget jokes now, though she was legitimately a little offended.

Bridget admits, though, that she too had changed and could no longer devote the same level of time to her best friend. In 2006, when Sophie was six months and growing, Bridget was busy with her final year of school and heading for her next stage of life. She was busier than ever, involved in every activity known to a zealous senior student – the school musical, debate, mediation, netball, rugby league and basketball – and she and Jan coached a basketball team together, yet another weekly activity at which Sophie was always a regular spectator. The period was exciting, but also deeply scary for Bridget. She knew she was just lurch-ing towards the time when she would be leaving her highly functional small-town childhood for everything that was new and strange. There were endless parties and final hurrahs and the spectacle of the year, the prom, to which Jan arranged a vintage car to chauffeur Bridget and her mates.

But no amount of custom celebrations could put off the inevitable. The new year came and when the day for Bridget to move on finally hit, it hurt. 'I ended up leaving two weeks early because I just couldn't deal with any more goodbyes.' Even her siblings, Matthew and Ellen, who were already in Brisbane, where Bridget would be attending university, were a little unfamiliar – she was relieved that they were there but with the huge age gap, Bridget was still just considered 'the baby' in the family. Sophie seemed to feel the turmoil, as dogs do. The moment that she had been sensing, when Bridget would leave home, eventually came.

The day she left Mackay, Bridget packed the car at dawn with Jan's help and Luke came over with coffee for everyone. It was a rainy day in early February 2007. Luke and Dave stood in the driveway. Luke, who had joined the family business, chatted with his father about electrical jobs that were coming up and various bits of gossip, a distraction Dave appreciated. Dave watched out of the corner of his eye as Bridget, her face blotchy and stern, went about readying to leave. He was proud of her, but happy for Luke's chatter. Jan, who was accompanying Bridget to Brisbane, continually fussed around with last minute details. She was doing her best to keep from getting emotional. Crying was not her style; tending to domestic details filled that space.

Sophie, meanwhile, may as well have had her hands on her hips.

'She got in the car and she wouldn't get out,' remembers Bridget, who still tears up when she thinks about that day. 'She was like, *I know you're leaving and you're not coming back, therefore I'm not getting out of the car.*' Sophie plonked herself in the passenger seat while Bridget waited in the driver's seat, taking deep breaths, unable to say any more goodbyes to Dave and Luke. She grabbed Sophie, hugged her tightly and then tried to push her away. Sophie had her tail between her legs, not looking at Bridget – sulking but demanding. 'I was like, *just get down, just get down, I need to get out of here.*'

Sophie wouldn't budge. In the end, Dave had to grab the devoted dog and pull her by the collar, paws clinging to the car as he slid her out.

Bridget and Jan drove out of Mackay listening to the song Bridget had chosen for the occasion: Oasis' 'Half the World Away'. Neither of them looked back.

3

An Empty Nest, Some Sulking and a Griffith Dog Makes History

Sophie sulked for days. Her impressive appetite waned and she was not even rushing in for tidbits from the barbecue. She would still bound up, all smiles, to greet Jan and Dave when they got home, but afterwards she would drift out to stand at the top of the porch steps, where she had spent so many placid hours daydreaming with Bridget, and stare out dolefully, searching for her. She'd lie with her head between her paws, rolling her eyes up, seemingly without even the energy to lift her head. Jan and Dave started to worry as this continued for nearly a week, before Sophie, seeming to acknowledge that Bridget wasn't coming back anytime soon, began to regain her appetite for steak and socialising. One day she dropped a tennis ball at

Dave's feet as he sat out by the pool, and looked up at him with her tail wagging. It was as if to say, *OK, brooding time is over, let's have a game.*

Bridget's departure marked the end of an era for each member of the Griffith family. Both Dave and Jan were missing their youngest's lively presence around the house, but they were also proud parents, and were beginning to be able to relish the fact that the two of them had a lot to look forward to, themselves. All their hard work with the family business was paying off, they were living in one of the most beautiful places in the world, and they had Sophie.

For Jan, in particular, Sophie was a godsend. In the hurly-burly of Bridget's final year and the bustle leading up to her leaving, Jan had managed to avoid thinking too much about what life would be like once her youngest had left. Having cooked, mentored, tutored and been as active a parent as possible at the kids' schools since her first two were born in the seventies, Jan was now faced with a childless home. She had spent the last year of Bridget's schooling busier than she'd ever been, and that was how she liked it.

So when Jan arrived back in Mackay after helping the apprehensive Bridget get through her first few days of city life, she walked into the kitchen to a silence so deep she could almost hear the walls cracking. For days after, Jan felt really down. There was a massive hole in her life and she felt sluggish and anxious at the same time. She moped about wondering what to cook, whether to rearrange the living room furniture or to call the library and volunteer her time. Had she not had Sophie there, she might have plunged into a deeper gloom. 'The bottom fell out of my world,' Jan says.

Bridget was slowly absorbing the new freedom down in Brisbane but she was also feeling really homesick. She called, sometimes teary, and it was always the same thing. 'How's the dog?' Bridget would demand. Jan was almost reluctant to tell her how gorgeous Sophie was being, following her around and keeping her company. She also didn't want to tell Bridget that Sophie had sulked for days and that she clearly missed her. She didn't want to encourage Bridget's nostalgia. Nevertheless, Jan would walk out to the steps where Sophie was sleeping and put the phone up to the dog's ear.

'Sophie Tucker!' Bridget would sing into the phone and Sophie would cock her head and prick her ears up and down, looking all around to work out where the noise was coming from. Bridget could have gone on like this for a long time, but Jan felt responsible for helping her daughter move on to the next phase of her life. 'It was a bit pathetic, really,' Jan jokes now. 'I felt uncomfortable about her talking to a dog on the phone.'

For all her maternal eye rolling, though, it was at this time that Jan and Sophie started to really bond. With no Bridget around, and Dave either at work or down at the marina polishing *Honey May* and chatting to mates, Sophie now started to attach herself to Jan. And after a week or so, Jan realised that the only way she was going to beat the gloom was to get out of the house and start moving. She began to take Sophie on the walks that were usually Dave's domain. Late in the afternoon, they would take off to Mackay's Botanic Gardens and Jan's friends would see the two of them, walking along the road with Sophie pulling Jan, the pair in a sort of tug of war. Sophie bulldozed along the path, nose down, as Jan leaned her whole upper body back, attempting to maintain control while not messing with Sophie's posture. The normally gentle Sophie showed her brute side on these walks, as she perpetually tugged on the lead, at times frothing at the mouth just so she could go a little bit faster. The dog would be in pain, the lead digging into her as it muzzled her jaw, but none of it seemed to matter to Sophie or stop her from trying to go faster and further.

'She would absolutely not give up,' says Jan, who remembers that even wild Jordy was better behaved on the leash, realising after three or four walks of being constantly pulled into line by Luke or Dave that the choking and the frothing was just plain unpleasant. Not Sophie – she was not a gentle walker.

Gradually, Jan and Dave both began to adjust to their new reality. Yet, while the fun levels were slowly rising for the residents of the family home, Bridget was still struggling to detach from her hometown. She was calling every day and, in fact, it was only a few weeks after her departure when the Easter long weekend fell and Bridget was on a plane back to Mackay, where Jan met her at the airport. Jan was ecstatic to see her daughter again but nervous that it would further prolong Bridget's adjustment to her new life. The euphoria of independence wasn't quite taking hold of the baby of the family yet, and Jan worried that that was partly because things were so good for her at home.

Despite her concern, Jan was not going to skimp on homey treats for her daughter's return. The consummate mother busied about in the days leading up to the visit, baking up one of her famous lasagnes and Bridget's favourite iced apricot cake – there was enough food for several families of Griffiths.

The much-anticipated reunion between Bridget and Sophie was a moment worthy of daytime television. Jan drove Bridget through the gate on the Thursday evening before Good Friday, just as the sun began to turn orange and a slight breeze rocked the palm trees. The neighbours probably heard the squeals. Sophie was aware that something was going on in the days before, perking her ears up and down as she followed Jan, who was peppier and chattier than she'd been for a few weeks. And as Sophie coasted towards the car it took no time for her to figure out that it wasn't only Jan in there. Sophie began to grunt from the back of her throat and her wagging tail broke into a whole bottom wobble as Bridget opened the door and yelled, 'Sophie Tucker!' Sophie didn't have time to jump in the car, Bridget was out and picking the now fully-grown and sizeable Sophie up and swinging her around. Bridget was tearing up and Jan was shaking her head. 'Put her down, silly girl,' she said, nevertheless beaming.

Bridget didn't listen. She carried the dog around for most of the weekend. That evening, after standing at the kitchen island pinching slices of tomato and red onion from the salad Jan was preparing, she skipped out to the screen door where Sophie was looking in at them, picked her up and lugged her inside to sit on the kitchen floor while Jan cooked. Bridget sat with her long legs in front of her, cradling Sophie, whose legs splayed over Bridget's.

Dave stood at the kitchen door and shook his head at his daughter and his best buddy draping themselves all over each other. 'Pathetic,' he said, shaking his head. His eyes were shining in clear admiration.

The weekend went by with several late nights and lots of chats about university and Bridget's studies. Was she liking business and commerce, as Matthew had? Or did she still want to pursue acting, as she'd always wanted to? A combination would be better, Dave and Jan urged. Sophie stood by all the while, either pressed up against the screen door, content to be close to the action going on at the dining table, or flopped belly up, resting in the crook of Bridget's arm on the green leather couch in front of the television. Sophie was there when Bridget's friends came over for a swim and Sophie was there, standing once again in the driveway with soapy eyes, ears dropped and legs splayed apart, when Jan and Dave drove Bridget back out the gate on their way to the airport.

Bridget's visit – and several subsequent visits in quick succession thereafter – helped to temper everyone's new existential anxieties. Bridget moved on with her new life in Brisbane and Jan and Dave's routines began to take full advantage of all the good things their life had to offer. 'Another day in paradise,' is how Dave would greet his days in Mackay. From the kitchen window, he'd look out onto the giant poinciana tree in the backyard and marvel at the sun on the weeping fig tree next door. But not before a big slurp from Sophie, who would wake some mornings at six, and others at eight. Like a social adolescent, how early she stirred would depend on the sort of night she'd had before: whether she was taking in the atmosphere of one of Jan's famous dinner parties or, on most nights, simply hanging with Jan and Dave around the barbecue area or lying under their feet as they watched TV.

Most mornings, Sophie would nudge open the door to Jan and Dave's bedroom and pad around to Dave's side of the bed, claws clicking ever so gently on the hardwood floor. As Dave slept, Sophie would take a seat as close to the edge of the bed as she could get, her nose a matchbox away from Dave's. Then she would wait quietly. If Dave didn't wake in good time, Sophie would put a paw up and rest it on Dave's arm. Dave's eyes would open to look straight into Sophie's, whose tail would start wagging, and she'd turn to lead the way. As Dave would throw off the covers, she'd look back at him, her body directed towards the door. She'd lead a barefoot Dave out of the bedroom, passing by Jan who'd let out a sleepy, 'Hey, darlin',' scratching Sophie on the neck on her way by.

During the week, Sophie had her early mornings with Dave, fetching the *Daily Mercury* from the driveway and sitting beside him as he unwrapped and read it. Then Dave would head off to work and Sophie would go looking for Jan. The least favourite part of Sophie's days was around quarter to eight, when Jan, freshly perfumed and blonde bob casually blown dry would descend the steps with her handbag over one shoulder, keys in her right hand. Sophie knew what this meant: alone time. And Sophie was never happy about it. She'd stop wagging her tail and the patter of her paws on the concrete carport halted. She'd look up at Jan with sad eyes, a wrinkle between them, blinking. It broke Jan's heart every day as she clicked the remote to shut the gate behind her, leaving Sophie standing in the middle of the driveway, turning her head but clearly watching Jan drive away to work.

Jan would leave each morning for Dave Griffith Electrical to take care of financial and administrative matters (and gossip with Megan, Dave's personal assistant extraordinaire). But this was not before she stopped for breakfast in Oscar's café in the centre of Mackay. No more toast and marmalade and instant coffee at home. Jan became a latte-out-every-morning kinda gal the day Bridget left home.

'Jan was one of our first loyal customers,' says owner John Flanagan, whose wife, Lauren, has known Jan since her teens. Jan would always come into the café looking crisp and colourful, her shoes usually matching some other element of her outfit, be it a necklace or a stripe on her sweater. As the kids had left, Jan increasingly lived the big-city lifestyle in her small town, driving around in a sleek silver Nissan 350Z that turned every seventeen-year-old male's head when Jan zoomed past, lippy on, blonde hair done. Jan says she doesn't care about cars the way she does shoes and outfits, but Dave had told her that they deserved to have a little bit of fun in their retirement years. 'And it is fun,' she admits.

Some days, Jan would breakfast on her own. She'd chat with the waitresses, usually Europeans or Canadians on working holidays, or join Desley, a septuagenarian artist with incredible skin and a storied single life. Most days, Dave would join Jan after stopping in at the office to assess the day and to catch up with Luke and the 'sparkies'.

The walls of Oscar's café are lined with photos of Hollywood greats: Marilyn Monroe, James Cagney, Lauren Bacall, Steve McQueen, Charlie Chaplin and a long-haired Brad. But there's another legend there, too: beside the coffee machine and above the cakes in the glass cabinet hangs a framed newspaper article about Griffo and his mates in their heyday as surfers, showing a twenty-something Dave with a washboard stomach riding a wave on a long board, white shirt ripped from left shoulder to right hip. John slyly 'borrowed' this picture when he was round at Jan and Dave's at a dinner party.

After spending time at the office, Jan would return home by lunchtime to be greeted by Sophie as the gate opened, the dog's whole behind sashaying and a squeaky pork chop, one of the pup's favourite toys, in her mouth. As Jan would turn into the driveway, Sophie would always be waiting, eager to drop the pink rubber thing at Jan's feet as she opened the car door. 'Hello, sweetheart,' Jan would say, and Sophie would look up at her and move her tongue in and out a few times.

After lunch, Jan might get the brush out for one of Sophie's favourite pastimes. Sophie couldn't resist when Jan or Dave brushed her, curling in towards them, a pup lapping up the love from her family. Add a tennis ball to the mix and Sophie would be in heaven, slobbering on it gently, lifting a paw or spreading her hind legs in complete submission as she was brushed.

In her quiet time, Sophie would lie for hours, belly squashed up against a fence or a tree, in the exact spot where the sun beamed down. Sometimes Jan would look through the shutters of the upstairs room to see Sophie standing over the pool, looking out across it as the sounds of a car entering the street or a distant dog barking grabbed her attention.

Later, Sophie would have her cheerful afternoon routine with Dave. Dave would take her for neighbourhood walks, which were a vigorous affair. He relished the exercise, and was always charmed by Sophie's eagerness to get out there, and then her enthusiasm to stop for a pee or to say hello to a stranger. No matter what the weather, even in the middle of wet-season storms, Dave and Sophie had their walks. Jan's friends would sometimes see Dave in his yellow raincoat, his balding head ploughing through the rain down the road as Sophie strode forward, tail and ears on alert. Sometimes, though, it was just too chaotic outside for walking. With gutters rushing and muddy puddles all over the paths and lawns, Jan would say, 'It's not walking weather.' Dave might privately agree but would still look at Sophie and shrug his shoulders. 'Sorry, mate, the boss has said the word.' For the rest of the afternoon, Dave would intermittently mutter that Sophie must be hating him just then.

When the pair came home from their long walks, Sophie would lap up water from her big red plastic bowl under the stairs in the carport while Dave cracked open his first Corona for the day and sliced a bit of lemon to squeeze it in. After a short break for refreshments, he and Sophie, excited to be off her lead, would then jog off to the empty grass block next door where she could run and roll and sniff around the weeping fig and mango trees to her heart's content.

Some days, Dave's neighbour from across the back fence would bring his bull terriers to run around with Sophie. The group of burly dogs would run and chase each other and bark, wrestling and pouncing and yelping, throwing slobber and paws into the air. If the neighbour wasn't home to bring the dogs out, Sophie would make a beeline for the fence behind which they waited for their owner. She'd sniff them out, nose to the ground, and as she heard the barks begin, she'd run up and down alongside the fence, as if to say, *I'm out here, why aren't you guys? Think what fun we could be having*!

Weekends, both Jan and Dave would be at home and Sophie would have non-stop companionship. Dave would spread out every national newspaper on the table under the house and spend hours reading them and snoozing in the sun. Sophie would be there, by his side, sometimes slinking under his chair to curl up in the shade and get some sleep, other times bringing him a tennis ball and politely dropping it at his feet when she was in the mood for a game. With her placid, self-contained nature, Sophie was content as long as there were people and activity around her.

It was something Matthew and his wife Melissa commented on when they came home from Brisbane for holidays and sat downstairs to catch up on life with Jan and Dave. They told stories of Bridget's exploits, as she was becoming a bit of a regular at the couple's Friday night TV footy gatherings. It reassured Jan and Dave to know that the three of their children who had moved away had each other to call on. As the four of them sat around chatting, with tea and a slice of Jan's banana cake, Sophie sauntered over to Matthew and rested her chin on his lap.

'Wow,' Matthew remarked, a little melted. He was used to Jordy, who had nipped and bitten his friends over the years.

'She's lovely, isn't she? She's different from our other dogs.'

Sophie never wanted to be anywhere but with the family. As the Griffiths chatted and joked and Jan offered around more snacks, Sophie moved from one visitor to the next, nuzzling her nose onto Melissa's lap and looking up at her with tender brown eyes.

'Hello,' Melissa replied to Sophie, scratching her under the chin. Then she turned to Jan, who was looking on in open adoration of her pet. 'You're right – she's just totally gorgeous, isn't she?'

As Sophie began to enjoy more and more of Dave and Jan's attention in the weeks and months after Bridget's departure, the idea that dogs belonged outdoors started to seem a little harsh. Both Jan and Dave missed the naughty evenings when Bridget nursed Sophie on her lap in front of the TV. And it wasn't long before Dave couldn't bring himself to look through the screen door into Sophie's adoring eyes and say goodnight if it was raining or there was a cold snap coming through Mackay. He'd step outside and Sophie would look at him, groan lovingly, snort and lie on her back as he rubbed her chest or stroked her between the eyes. She would never try to nudge her way in uninvited.

This all took a toll on the oh-so-tough Dave, who missed both his daughters terribly, now that neither was around to joke with and occasionally pamper. There was a lot of friendly teasing between Dave and the two Griffith sisters. Dave might shake his head about how many new dresses or hairstyles they came home with – usually after a shopping trip with Jan – but he'd always offer his honest, considered opinion. He was not a fan of short hair so an ongoing joke between Ellen and Bridget was that Ellen, with her long thick tresses, was the favourite, as Bridget had been sporting a pixie do for several years. He still encouraged Jan to grow her blonde bob out again, the way he always loved it. 'She thinks she's too old or something,' he'd say, with his side smile.

Now Dave's affection for his daughters got channelled almost entirely into Sophie. The two of them spent a lot of time together out by the pool. If Dave sat down, Sophie would gently put her head on his lap and he would pat her, the two of them sitting there and looking at each other for minutes at a time. If Dave emptied the skimmer box on the pool, Sophie would be right beside him. She'd have her head slightly down as if listening out for vibrations in the ground, and her tail would wag every so often. Her ears would be up and she would sniff the rubbish that came out of the box, curiously, and then go and sniff it again when Dave threw it into the garden. 'She was so interested in everything he did,' says Jan.

When Matthew or Ellen called Jan, weekly and sometimes daily, just to check in and catch up, the older Griffith siblings would always ask how Sophie was and be regaled with stories about how she was currently flopping by Dave's side as he read a newspaper, or that she'd just performed a new trick that Dave had encouraged.

Several months after Bridget left home, as the evenings wound down and Jan was getting ready for bed, Dave started to bring up the idea that perhaps they could let Sophie inside on those cold nights. She could just sleep on the mat behind the front door and then they wouldn't have to worry about her shivering on her own, outdoors. And he wouldn't have to get up so early to check on her.

'Think how much happier she'd be on the mat,' he'd tell Jan, who took a little convincing.

'So much for his "she's a cattle dog, she should be outside under an old corrugated iron water tank",' she'd jive.

Jan had always taken pride in steering a course as a pet owner between parental affection and respectful distance. Cattle dogs aren't sissies. They are a sturdy, competent, self-possessed breed, built to work in Australia's fierce heat for days on end and control animals that could crush them with one hoof. 'It's important that we give them their dog dignity – they are dogs and cattle dogs especially. There's that line in the sand that they draw themselves. They are your dog and you look after them, but you have to respect their dogginess. It's not all "oochy coochy coochy, baby, baby baby." You can't call a dog "baby",' says Jan.

So while Dave affected an air of authoritarianism it was in fact he, not Jan, who led the Griffith family transition from steadfast canine disciplinarians to utter softies.

Of course, the always very polite Sophie needed some coaxing to be convinced that she was welcome inside the house. The first time she was invited in, she was completely coy. She slinked along the ground, bending her legs and creeping inside, butt practically dragging on the hardwood floors. As Dave and, eventually, Jan were inviting her in, they'd bend down and woo her, clicking their tongues and assuring her, 'it's all right sweetheart, come inside.' As she inched towards the red Turkish rug in front of the TV, she wouldn't look them in the eye. Her ears were back, tail between her legs as Dave persuaded her. 'Come on, Tuck, come inside.'

So much for tough love. Eventually, Sophie became more comfortable with the idea that she was an inside dog. And she was making Griffith history: never before had a family dog made it this far.

It took a few weeks, but in the end Sophie went from comfortable to cocky. Some nights when he couldn't sleep and came out to check on her, Dave would catch her stretched out on an old low-sitting leather armchair with wooden arms almost as wide as Sophie was long. She wouldn't turn to him or whip her tail in greeting; she was feeling too guilty. Sometimes she'd just catch his eye as she slid herself off the chair. But she'd been invited on to the rug, and the taste for domestic comfort had become addictive. It didn't take long for the armchair to become Sophie's.

Sophie loved her rug, came to revel in her armchair and especially relished the newfound comfort of being out of Mackay's wet-season summer days. Though Mackay locals roll their eyes at the assumption that the city's on a par with the extreme tropical climates of further north Queensland, it can rain for days and weeks at a time and is often twenty-nine or thirty degrees; for a dog with a substantial fur coat, Mackay is rather warm.

When lying in the sun got too much, Sophie would saunter up the stairs and Jan and Dave would say, 'Are you hot, darlin'?' They'd open the screen door for her to flop inside. She'd drop, belly on the hardwood floor, absorbing the impact of the air conditioner that was set to a delicious twenty-three degrees.

When Luke came over for veal schnitzel, his favourite of Jan's meals, the sight of Sophie regally sitting up on her green leather armchair made him slightly indignant. 'What's this?' he'd exclaim. Not only had his Jordy never been allowed inside, she was never even allowed to climb the stairs up to the screen door. If she put so much as two paws on the bottom step, Dave would yell at her, 'Get downstairs!'

Sometimes Sophie would look at Luke from her armchair, sheepishly, her head hanging a little, seemingly aware that, yes, she was getting special treatment. If Luke came over early in the morning on his way to work and caught Sophie flopped out and still sleeping on the armchair, just the tip of her tail would whip a little on the chair, like a child giggling in the knowledge that it's getting away with something naughty.

Luke found this state of affairs sort of endearing, but also appalling.

'I still bitch about it,' admits Luke, for whom the scenario further reaffirms his little sister's golden-child status.

And after several weeks of this, it began to get hard for Jan to usher Sophie outside in the mornings when she was leaving for her latte on the way to work.

'Sophie, come on!' she'd call, standing in the doorway, keys in one hand, holding the screen door open with the other. Sophie would open her eyes and lift her head. You've got to be joking, said her eyes. *It's hot out there.*

Jan would have to close the screen door, walk over to Sophie and tell her, 'You are coming outside,' before nudging her with her foot, at which point Sophie would finally heave herself up. But Dave was enamoured with his girl and not about to shoo her from this new comfort zone.

In actual fact, Jan and Dave never regretted letting Sophie into the house because she was just so well-behaved. As an inside dog, Sophie was a delight. When she needed to go out, she'd never scratch at the door, whimper or bark. Instead, she'd meander over and stand there patiently, looking out the door soberly, head slightly down as if stopped mid-motion. She'd wait for someone to work it out. If too much time passed, she'd turn her head around to see where everyone was. Jan would often come out of the kitchen to find Sophie sitting there, a slightly mournful expression on her face, looking up at Jan. 'She's thinking, *let me out, you drongo,*' Jan laughs. '*Let me out. I'm not going to spell it out.*'

When Jan and Dave were watching TV, Sophie would lie down in front of the television with her two paws crossed. She'd lay her head on one paw or look up and around, making sure everyone was still there, surveying the scene with genuine but by no means needy interest.

And so, as Sophie, going on two years old and vibrant as ever, moved from the top of the steps to the armchair, she was moving up the pecking order from family pet to fifth child, a child that needed little else but love and a few raw bones (and a Turkish rug). She also became an unofficial caretaker. The gorgeous Sophie Tucker played a central role in offsetting any fears Jan and Dave had about entering their golden years, and any guilt their children might have had about no longer living at home. The Griffith children gathered great comfort in knowing that Jan and Dave weren't home alone: they had their girl.

4

All Aboard Honey May –
Sophie and the Family Go Boating

The initial decision to take Sophie on the boat, all of them admit, was Dave and Bridget's, and it was made one Saturday night while they were all aboard *Honey May*. Bridget, now in her second year at uni, was home for the holidays and the three Griffiths decided to have an overnight stay on the boat, which was docked down at the Mackay Marina. The family sat around on *Honey May*'s deck and several neighbours stopped by for a glass of beer or wine throughout the evening. The three Griffiths ate Thai takeaway and decided that they were having so much fun and the weather was so beautiful, they'd extend this little boat adventure and take *Honey May* for a ride out of the harbour the next day.

At around ten, Jan went off to bed below deck. Meanwhile, Dave and Bridget moved into one of their infamous Dave-and-Bridget evenings, a tradition wherein Bridget returns home from university and Dave walks around with his head in his hands, groaning the next day. On this night in 2008, father and daughter sat drinking Coronas with lemon, reminiscing and exchanging jokes. It wasn't much before midnight, the music still blasting from the Sails Sports Bar up at the marina, when Bridget and Dave's conversation turned to Sophie, who at that time was just two years old.

'What are we going to do with that bloody blue thing?' Dave asked in his characteristic faux gruff tone. 'She'll be sulking when we go home, and she won't like being left tomorrow, either.'

That afternoon, as the family had busied about the house, packing picnic and party gear into the Nissan, a dejected Sophie lay on the concrete floor in a corner near the laundry, her head slumped between her toes. She knew they were leaving her, she'd experienced this plenty of times before and she wasn't going to wag her tail about it. She pretended she wasn't interested in their doings but every so often, she squeezed her eyes open to sneak peeks at the family action.

'Why don't we just bring her with us?' Bridget exclaimed, clinking another two Coronas together as she pulled them from the fridge in the kitchen below deck. 'Let's tell Mum we're going to bring her along.'

Bridget was so excited about the prospect she insisted

they wake Jan and tell her that very night. Jan was only half asleep, as the sounds of all the fun being had outside were carrying into the bedroom. She heard shuffling in the saloon and then Bridget whisper, 'Mum?' She opened her eyes to find Dave and Bridget standing over her, cheeky expressions on both their faces.

'We're bringing Sophie with us tomorrow,' Bridget announced. Jan, eyebrows raised, looked at Dave, who looked back at his wife with resignation. *It was your daughter's idea, I swear*, his expression indicated.

'She'll love it!' Bridget insisted. 'Imagine how happy we'll make her.'

Jan shook her head with mock disapproval, looked at her husband and her youngest child matter-of-factly and said, 'She's both of your responsibilities.' Jan was secretly thrilled, and they all knew it.

The next morning, Bridget left Jan and Dave on *Honey May* and drove back to the house to pick up an ecstatic Sophie, who was waiting on the driveway when she arrived and wagged her tail in triple time when she realised that Bridget had come home to pick her up.

'Come on, girl! We're going on the boat!' Bridget yelled, clapping her hands, excited as if it was she who was going out on the boat for the first time, not Sophie. She picked up Sophie's front paws and the two did a little dance, then they jogged down the driveway back to the car and Bridget drove back to the marina with Sophie in the front passenger seat, tongue out. Bridget walked an exuberant Sophie on her lead to the locked marina gate. As Bridget swiped the entry card, Sophie could not be contained. She could see Jan on the deck of *Honey May* three rows down and she bolted, ripping her lead from Bridget's grip. She galloped down the ramp, ears back, lead flying out behind her. Jan looked up from where she was fussing about on deck to see Sophie with her tongue flapping out bounding towards her, and Bridget in shorts and sunglasses bouncing on her nose, running behind crying, 'I can't hold her!'

Jan flung her arms out wide and yelled, 'Sophie Tucker!'

As Sophie rounded the corner of the deck to *Honey May*, she skidded, her paws straightening out, readying for the jump into and beyond Jan's arms. 'I was clapping and she was coming towards me excited as anything,' Jan gleefully remembers. 'She was just so happy to be there. It was fantastic.'

As Dave steered the boat out of the harbour, leaving the coal ships of Mackay behind for the island-scattered blue ocean, Sophie stood by Jan and Bridget, tongue lolling, her whole rump wagging, looking around and back at them, as if to say, *look, there's the ocean!* After years of larking and splashing about in the shallows, now here she was, adventuring much farther than her beloved beach. Delighted to be with her family on a new adventure, she was hungrily lapping up the sensation of spray on her face, and fierce wind through her ears.

For the Griffiths, emerging from the headlands with

the wake of the boat spreading and boiling was always the first thrill on their boating trips. It was the moment when the industrial shoreline of Mackay gave way to the Great Barrier Reef Marine Park, which has been referred to as 'the oceanic equivalent of the Amazon rainforest.' The neck of the Mackay Marina opens out to the wide ocean, which even on rough days is layered with glassy blues, and the most southern of the islands comes into view. People in Mackay try to knock off work at four in the afternoon so they can hoon around on jet skis, kayaks and boats, in order to spend their weekends in the thick of the marine wilderness on their doorstep. It takes about an hour or so to boat to a smattering of primitive islands, including St Bees and Keswick, which are part of the South Cumberland Islands, south of the Whitsundays. These islands are not littered with catered resorts, but instead are barely touched pockets of land with just a handful of dwellings, perhaps a picnic area, and thickets of tropical plant life to lie and snooze under.

'When you're out there, something happens that just makes you go, "wow",' Jan says. Sophie seemed to appreciate it, too. As Dave pushed up *Honey May*'s speed and the motor roared, Sophie started panting and raised her nose high into the air, seemingly thrilled to be included in the newest family adventure.

Honey May was small for a motor cruiser and required her crew to be quite cautious while on board, especially when the boat was moving. Dave's rule was that passengers decided where they wanted to be – at the front, the back or up on the flybridge with the driver – before they left the marina, so there was not too much moving back and forth while the boat was in motion. The sides of the boat were very narrow, and getting from the bow to the stern required a walking-sideways manoeuvre while holding tight onto the thin metal railing. The front of the boat was most comfortable and scenic. It got choppy the further out you went and the faster the boat was travelling, and while a better vantage point was to be had up on the flybridge, the wind was always wilder, so if the family decided to ride up there when the boat was in full throttle, it was all sightseeing and contemplation, not conversation. And wherever the passengers chose to travel, safety was everybody's top priority. 'It's a boat,' Dave would say to Jan. 'We cannot take any chances. We take everyone's life into our hands when we're on board.'

On this beautiful Sunday morning, the perfect setting for Sophie's maiden voyage, Bridget and Jan sat up at the front with their backs to the window, their legs stretched out and sunhats secured tightly to prevent them blowing off. Sophie sat between them, where they could hang on to her. Often, they'd wear waterproof jackets to avoid getting their clothes soaking wet from the waves, but on this occasion, everyone was enjoying the spray. Especially Sophie, who discovered that this fabulous adventure also allowed her another chance at her childhood game: catching water in her jaws. She took a snap every now and again on that first trip, lifting her head and licking at the water spray as it splashed over them. For most of the time, Sophie sat calmly, the wind in her face and the sun on her blue and grey coat, her tongue hanging out in glee. She seemed to be soaking up this new experience, figuring out what it was all about. *So this was what her family got up to when they left her at home.*

Bridget and Jan watched her in adoration. 'What do you think, Sophie Tucker?' Jan, squinting, called out to her over the noise of the engine.

'How cool is this, Tuck?' Bridget joked, grabbing the pup around the shoulders in a gesture that combined affection and protection.

The family boated out to one of their favourite places on earth, Scawfell Island. Scawfell is the largest of the Cumberland Islands, just twenty-five nautical miles from their front door. The Griffiths were planning to moor in the island's only anchorage, Refuge Bay, a pristine inlet of mottled blue water that laps onto a ribbon of white sand.

Those in the know regard the island as a kind of sacred place. Scawfell consists, for the most part, of mountains thickly covered in green, edged around with red and grey granite boulders that turn a deep orange during winter sunsets. The boulders come in dramatic shapes, some propped on top of each other by just one edge, and seemingly about to topple. The Mackay-based rangers who travel over there for security and maintenance dream about having time to traipse over these boulders and through the thick vegetation that clings to the mountains.

Not quite an hour and a half after they left the harbour, Dave finally slowed the boat down and Sophie began to trot on the spot as she watched Jan and Bridget edge about, helping Dave to anchor.

'Stay there, Tucker,' Dave called out to her as he pointed to Bridget to throw him a rope. 'How are you, girl?' he said, turning back to Sophie, remembering even in his haste to make anchor that this was a momentous occasion in his Sophie's life. Sophie looked at him, all dog smiles. She sniffed around and watched their every step, waiting to be invited to move anywhere. She seemed to know that the rules on the boat were different from those back at home.

The Griffiths pulled out their deck chairs and prepared to spend a lazy afternoon on *Honey May*. Dave fidgeted with the engine in its hatch at the back of the main deck while Jan got the lunch together down in the tiny galley kitchen two short levels below deck. It was equipped with a mini fridge and a stove, just a few cramped steps from the shower and toilet.

Meanwhile, Bridget showed Sophie around. 'Come on Soph!' she called, tempted to pick her up, but she knew that Dave would not approve. Sophie needed to get used to making her way around the rocking boat.

Bridget escorted the frisky pup along the side of the boat, talking her through it as she, herself, hung on to the rail and watched Sophie trot obediently and gingerly behind her. Bridget took Sophie to the glass door that opened down to the saloon where she would sleep with Bridget later that night, once the faux-leather booth had been folded out into a guest bed. Three steps farther down below deck was the forward cabin – the closest thing *Honey May* got to a master bedroom. Jan and Dave slept there in the V-shaped berth, their legs hitting the walls and criss-crossing up against each other.

'It wasn't comfortable,' says Jan. 'But you didn't care when you were out there.'

'It was a bastard,' says Dave, reminding Jan that they had to step on a milk crate to get into bed. It was above this space, up on the front deck, that Sophie sunbaked later that afternoon alongside Bridget and Jan. The Griffith women sat around in wide-brimmed hats, Bridget in a bikini, reading novels and doing crosswords, while Dave flipped through newspapers and looked over his map books, always learning about the marine area that was so much more accessible to him now that they had *Honey May.*

Later, Dave put steaks and sausages on the barbecue and Jan opened a bottle of wine she'd brought from her fridge at home. But this wasn't another big night. The mood was mellow, and so was Sophie, even in her enthusiasm. She had already sniffed around the boat a bit with Bridget and, having acquainted herself with the space, stuck pretty close to the family. As people moved in and out of the kitchen, preparing the meal, she sat on the top step but didn't go farther inside: her paws would slip and slide on the polished floors.

Sophie was very lively and seemed to be invigorated by the salt air. But she didn't seem to be in any way perturbed by being somewhere so unfamiliar. As they ate, Bridget and Jan on their deck chairs and Dave leaning up against the railing on the front deck, Sophie sat between them, looking back and forth and waiting for what she knew would come: meat scraps and maybe a potato skin or two.

When it came to bedtime, not long after the sun went down, Sophie had to be coaxed down to the cabin. In theory she was sleeping on the floor alongside Bridget, who of course invited her up to share the bed for the night.

The next morning, as coffee brewed, the family got ready to jump off the back of *Honey May* for a swim. The moment Sophie realised what was happening, as first Dave, then Bridget plunged into the water, she started barking wildly, overexcited at the realisation that her turn must be coming next. Jan needed to give her a little bit of gentle encouragement to take the plunge, but Bridget was treading water below and calling to her. She jumped. And she was ecstatic. She swam around and around in circles making her way towards Bridget and then Dave, her head stretched above the waves, mouth firmly shut to avoid taking in water.

The sun was up over Scawfell, its palm trees and boulders were starting to sparkle and the tips of the reefing coral were still visible as the tide was coming in. The risk of rips and swelling tides, as well as stinging and even lethal creatures, was far higher here than when Sophie ran into the waves off the beaches off Mackay, but the Griffiths weren't too concerned: the water in the bay was so clear and crisp and they swam in it all the time. It felt very safe. And Sophie was having the time of her life paddling about.

'Sophie!' Bridget yelled out to her and Sophie would paddle over to her, head stretched far out of the water, mouth scrunched up in zeal to get where she wanted to go. Bridget's tongue was practically hanging out like a dog's as she giggled and splashed Sophie.

'You lunatics,' Jan teased as she floated about on her back.

Sophie huffed and puffed through her nose, swishing around Bridget, and Bridget did somersaults in the water and sang out, 'Isn't this the bee's knees, Tucker?' Sophie moved her legs strongly, swerving around between Dave and Bridget. *Absolutely*, she seemed to be thinking.

The Griffiths were in for fifteen minutes or so before they decided it was breakfast time. Jan was already back on deck and towelling off, getting ready to prepare the meal

'Come on girls,' she said, looking out at Bridget and Sophie still swirling about. Dave swam over to the boat and readied to hoist himself up the ladder. Bridget ignored them and Sophie followed suit, moving round and round in circles, ready for another game. Jan went below deck and put the kettle on and started bringing out eggs and bread for the barbecue.

'Bridge!' Dave called. 'Sophie's going to be exhausted.'

But Sophie wasn't showing any signs of tiring. Dave went to grab Sophie to help her back up the ladder to the boat. Just as she had refused to budge from the car on the day of Bridget's departure to university, now she was refusing to cooperate with Dave and leave the ocean. He had to pretty much haul her up the ladder. Her eyes reproached him for cutting short her fun. *I'm a water dog,* she seemed to be saying. *Leave me be.*

The success of Sophie's first boat trip was a huge relief for Jan and Dave, who had worried that they'd acquired two incompatible but very much loved elements of their move into retirement: the freedom of an ocean cruiser and the responsibility that comes along with the joy of a dog. They'd worked hard to create a later life that encompassed them both and they wanted to enjoy the tropical paradise in which they'd established their family home.

The purchase of *Honey May* was not a light decision. Dave had had small boats throughout his life, and grown up around the ocean. When the children were younger, he spent every Sunday sailing off Mackay with mates on their catamarans, while Jan and the kids barbecued with other families on the shore. And when the Griffiths bought their beach house at Louisa Creek, forty minutes from Mackay, when Matthew and Ellen were teenagers, Dave bought a small catamaran; he'd really wanted a cruiser for a long time.

In the years leading up to the family's investment in *Honey May*, Dave spent much of his spare time educating himself: he read about navigation systems and engines and asked other skippers in the marina about operating boats and reading tides and charts, the weather and ocean channels. He taught himself to drive a boat and to maintain it. And he and Jan discussed whether investing in a machine that many people might consider a luxury, was justified. When they finally went ahead and bought *Honey May*, Dave was overjoyed. His only moment of worry had been on that morning, more than two years ago now, when he thought Jan was having second thoughts about the boat. But that turned out to be the joyful day that Sophie came into their lives. And now, Sophie, like the rest of the Griffiths, was learning to love the open ocean, thanks to *Honey May*.

When Dave planned a trip on the boat, he checked the forecasts vigilantly, studying several websites and taking notes. The Griffiths wouldn't go out if the weather was predicted to be anything less than perfect.

'You're always nervous,' Dave says of being a skipper, remembering his first times taking Jan, then the kids, and then friends out on the boat. 'There's a little sticker everywhere saying, *you're the driver, you are responsible.* You're standing up on the flybridge and looking at thirty-odd foot of boat in front of you and it's scary. Jan wouldn't come with me for a while.'

Dave saw it as part of his role as skipper to teach the rest of the family about the boat, and the magical but dangerous environment they had the good fortune to be able to explore. 'He creates this experience every time we go out; he really loves showing people the ocean,' Bridget says.

As Dave would drive the boat out of the headland, he'd point out ripples and swells in the ocean surface, and symbols on the GPS system. The aim was to familiarise everyone with hazards such as boulders and rough or shallow areas. 'Oi, Luke,' he'd call down to the main deck often and point out a rip or a rock, or sit up on the flybridge to teach them to read the sky and the ocean and to absorb the sense of concentration that it took to skip. 'It's all very well to have everything on auto but you don't just then go downstairs and read a book,' he says.

From their very first few trips he would make sure to bring Jan, Bridget and Luke up to the wheel to give them a rundown of the throttles and levers and monitors, drumming into their heads that the main thing to remember about steering a boat was that, unlike a car, the back always moved first. 'You can read all the books you like but at the end of the day, it's only practice that will do it,' he'd tell them. Dave wanted to inspire his children to learn to drive the boat so that it really was a family venture, and to make sure that Jan, who admitted to being a nervous Nelly on board, felt competent, herself, and didn't have to rely on him. It was Dave's dream for the boat to be a second home, and the effort was always worth it when the family was out on the water watching the fog roll in over the saddle of an island's mountains, dropping anchor to fish or jumping off the back of the boat to swim in a secluded bay.

Out on the ocean, Dave would often look back to Jan, who would be huddled behind him with a cap on and often a raincoat, looking out across the wheel, taking in the sea air with lips in a satisfied purse. They'd hold each other's gaze for a while, acknowledging, *We're doing it, sweetheart. We're living the life.*

In the winter, when Jan wasn't trying to will away her seasickness – sometimes it could be so bad she'd have to spend an hour hanging over the edge – she'd be squinting and craning her neck on the lookout for whales, which the family had seen many times, and which Jan describes as 'a spiritual experience.' Jan and Bridget would gasp and exclaim, 'Oh my God,' Jan with her hands over her mouth, Bridget with mouth wide open as they saw in the distance the whip of a blue tail. 'Even from far away, when you see one of them jump straight up in the air, and come down in a huge waterfall, it's the most incredible thing,' says Jan. 'Sometimes you feel that they know you're there and they're performing.'

None of this magic was ever lost on the Griffith kids. On their first trips out on the boat, as they moved beyond the headlands, Jan would say to Bridget, 'Aren't we the luckiest sons of guns in the world?'

'This is so cool,' Bridget would agree, and snap a

photo of a mussy-haired Jan against a cloudless sky, or turn the camera on herself and pull a silly face. Bridget would bring her Brisbane city friends up to Mackay for boat trips, and Luke and his girlfriend Heather had their boat licence, after hours and hours of driving around the harbour and parking the boat in and out of her narrow berth.

None of it seemed to be lost on Sophie, either. She was as much a water baby as Bridget and Luke. In the months that followed that first trip, Sophie got her sea legs and accompanied Dave and Jan whenever they went on the boat. She became a sea dog even more quickly than she'd taken to luxuriating on the leather armchair after Bridget left. She no longer sulked when she saw towels and straw hats and Jan's green canvas picnic basket being stashed into the back of the Nissan – she followed Jan and Dave around with glee. The sound of paws skipping along behind them on the carport became the sound of their pre-trip preparation.

For day and overnight visits, Jan would load up *Honey May* with meat for the barbecue, cans of Diet Coke for Jan's seasickness, avocadoes, fresh lettuce and tinned vegetables for Jan's Toowoon Bay salad (corn, peas and beetroot all from cans, with mayo on the side, based on a Griffith family joke about the sort of cooking Dave was raised on. When Dave would be home alone for a few nights while Jan visited one of the kids in Brisbane, Ellen and Bridget would tell Jan, 'Just leave him a can opener. He'll be right.'). And when the Griffiths swiped

Sophie Tucker

Matthew with 'Mack', Jan, Luke and Ellen with 'Tina' at Louisa Creek, 1985.

The neighbourhood dogs run alongside Dave on the tractor at Louisa Creek, 1985.

Matthew, Luke and Ellen with Sally's puppies, 1983. Matthew holds 'Mack'.

Dave at Shelley Beach, NSW, 1963, as seen in the newspaper clipping in Oscar's café.

Sophie as a curious little pup in 2006. Her ears seem bigger than she is.

I don't really like getting my picture taken, Sophie seems to be thinking.

Dave and a young Sophie play a game with the hose.

Sophie chases a ball in the backyard, 2007.

Bridget, home on holiday, with Sophie before bed-time.

Dave and Sophie after their walk.

The Griffiths' family home.

Honey May in Egremont Passage.

Bridget and Sophie in *Honey May*'s tender.

Sophie at the beach, wading after her swim with Bridget.

On the Keswick road where Brian Kinderman first encountered Sophie in the buggy.

Keswick airstrip.

View from the Keswick Island Guest House.

Arthur Bay, Keswick, at low tide.
Keswick residents saw Sophie's paw prints in this area.

St Bees Island above left, Keswick Island below.

View from Keswick over the narrow but treacherous Egremont Passage,
which Sophie swam across to reach St Bees.

their members' card to the marina gate, Sophie knew the drill: her lead was still on but the path down to *Honey May* was like an Olympic doggy run.

As they got out deep into the ocean, Sophie was always at one of their sides, eager to explore but most happy just to be with her crew. While Jan or Bridget sunbathed at the front of the boat, she lay beside them, the ocean breeze in her fur. She always assumed the same posture: nose raised in the air and mouth open, gulping in those sea odours and watching intently as the big sea birds circled overhead. Sophie accompanied the Griffiths on day trips north, up and around Cockermouth Island or over to St Bees, where the family would stay with Sophie onboard or in the tender, as dogs weren't allowed on shore.

Just as Sophie liked to wake Jan and Dave on land, she would begin her days on *Honey May* by trotting over to the door of their cabin around eight in the morning, already extra eager to get going: she knew something about the adventures that lay before her in boatland and they were even more exciting than the garden and air conditioning-based adventures back at home in Mackay. On *Honey May*, Jan and Dave would wake immediately to the sound of her paws outside the door to the lower cabin – though she would never descend the steps because of the slippery polished floors. Boater Sophie was a little less mellow than at-home Sophie.

While her sleepy owners stirred and got into their swimming gear, Sophie would jump into the small dinghy at the back of the boat and hop around, panting, occasionally barking, barely able to contain herself for the prospect of Jan and Dave motoring around the island and jumping in for a swim. She'd bark and she'd wriggle around. She loved being on the dinghy – even more so than being on *Honey May*. Perhaps it was the proximity to the water, the possibility of swimming. As Dave started the motor, Jan, in her floppy hat and sandals, would have to clutch Sophie – her hands sturdily grabbing Sophie's shoulders – until it was safe to let the wriggling pup free to jump out of the dinghy into the ocean where she could swim happily alongside them, head in the air, knowing there was an out if she needed it, unlike in the swimming pool.

Other times, they'd moor between islands, often out near Scawfell, where they'd spend the night, barbecuing and playing cards as the sun went down and dropping fishing lines in the water during the day, much to Sophie's delight. If Dave was ever too reserved to express his enthusiasm for this idyllic lifestyle, Sophie made up for it. Jan just had to look at her on the boat to be reminded that the nausea was all worth it.

Sophie took to boating with characteristic grace and seemed to complete the Griffith's vision of those empty-nesting days, paving their way towards retirement. 'She never minded what she was doing, as long as she was with us,' Dave says, though they could tell that being on the boat was one of Sophie's favourite activities. She'd radiate pure joy.

The Griffiths took a lot of trips in the second half of 2008, having spent the previous years getting their sea legs. One weekend, at the end of September 2008 when Bridget was home, the Griffiths were blessed with perfect boating weather. Dave had been watching the weather for the days leading up to Bridget's arrival and he liked what he was seeing. For a large percentage of the year, Mackay experiences prevailing south-easterly winds that are often more than ten to twelve knots, making boat trips more rugged than Jan liked, given her struggle with motion sickness. The winds make the water choppy and frothy and are very changeable, meaning a perfect day can quickly turn into a risky day. On rough days on the water, Jan spent a lot of her time following the advice given to people with motion sickness, hydrating and sitting very still with her hands clasped, looking steadfastly into the horizon.

When the weather reports start predicting decent five-knot winds, Mackay families like the Griffiths start preparing for glorious weekends out on the water. On the Friday before Bridget arrived, Jan and Dave ran around town buying bait for fishing and groceries for a barbecue, and Sophie was swept up in the giddiness of the activity around her, now that she was no longer afraid she was going to be left behind.

On the Saturday morning, the family, Sophie included, panting and tail wagging on Bridget's lap in the back seat, drove down to the marina at first light to get out on the water as quickly as possible and not waste a second of the fantastic conditions. As Dave drove the boat out of the marina, Bridget, Jan and Sophie perched on the flybridge. On that day, the horizon was the rich blue of a child's drawing and the spray created by *Honey May*'s motoring through the water was a delicate spritz, rather than the soaking, eye-stinging gusts it can be on rougher days. With Bridget on board they were able to get Sophie up to the flybridge. Dave and Bridget heaved her up the ladder as she submitted herself, ears back and eyes drooping, then once she was up there trotting around so happy to be included.

'Let's go fishing, Sophie Tucker!' Bridget sang, and ruffled Sophie around the head. They moored just outside Refuge Bay at Scawfell, alongside a handful of other boats with the same idea. They set up fishing lines and fussed about, ready to lounge in wait for a few bites. Dave looked over to see a couple of his work colleagues on a nearby boat and they all waved and yelled, 'What a day, hey?'

'Mate, beautiful.'

Sophie was sitting at the kitchen doorway, the end of her tail thumping on the step and her ears perking up and then down.

Because of the tightness of *Honey May*'s outdoor space, Sophie was relegated to the kitchen doorway when the family was fishing. From there she would watch, wagging and sniffing like mad when fish were pulled in over the edge. She loved the smell and the excitement as Bridget or Jan reeled in a frenzied coral trout or red throat emperor. If there was space, she'd venture out to approach a captured fish on the deck, moving her nose forward stealthily as if she were hunting a bird, but knowing this was not hers for the taking. 'She never got under our feet, she knew to keep her distance, but she'd very politely come forward for a sniff,' says Jan, proudly. 'And if the fish flapped around, she'd take a step back. It was just adorable.'

The pup couldn't always contain herself, though, and this day there were three lines on the go and one of them always had a fish on it. It was perfect fishing weather indeed and Jan and Bridget were getting girly, yelling with delight when every twenty minutes their lines tugged in their hands.

Dave spent most of his time keeping buckets out of the way and untangling Jan's line after she pulled in yet another metre-long coral trout. Dave kept a watch over Bridget's lines as she pulled in fish after fish, with the occasional near-miss of a tug on the line as she daydreamed for a second. All the while Sophie looked on in rapture.

'We were fishing on handlines,' Bridget remembers. 'Mum pulled in a fish and Sophie just had to come out to look at it.' As the pup trotted on to the deck, she got those paws all tangled in the fishing line. 'Dad's swearing his brains off,' says Bridget, 'Then I caught a fish and so there was another one coming in and Sophie was so excited.'

For Dave, though, the chaos was too much. 'Get inside,' he growled at the dog.

Sophie's ears perked up, then immediately dropped. She looked at Dave and over at Bridget's catch, flapping on the deck. But no amount of head cocking or sad eyes was going to sway Dave, the way it had when he'd found her on the leather armchair, promoting herself from the rug all those months ago. So Sophie went inside and plonked in a corner, sulking with her head between her front paws.

Her sulk didn't last long, though. As soon as Bridget was done fishing, she came inside and picked Sophie up, nuzzling her nose into the dog's chest, then putting her down so Sophie could go sniff the remnants of the fishing mission.

She might have been assigned to the sidelines of the fun that day but the Griffiths made up for it later, throwing her chunks of the barbecued coral trout that they ate with salad and bread whilst sitting around under the setting sun. The next morning it was fish again for breakfast, this time served with a fried egg. Sophie was in her element.

5

The Terrible Day –
Dog Overboard

Twenty-fifth October, the day they lost Sophie, is still almost too painful for the Griffith family to recall, but it began as just another morning in paradise. It was a Saturday, magical and sunny with yellow-bellied sunbirds singing in the Griffiths' back-yard, and Sophie waking Dave with a nudge of her I-need-to-go-out cold nose. Weather conditions for Saturday and Sunday were looking superb and the Griffiths had a lovely weekend planned.

Just a few weeks after Bridget's visit, Jan and Dave, still high on the perfection of that last bountiful fishing trip, were going to venture back over to Scawfell, where they hoped to meet their friends Denise and Ian Thomason who would be out there after a fishing competition.

Jan and Dave often took the tender over to the island to explore up the shore and meander around the bright coral under the trees and rocks that line the beach. They could be on the beach for hours and see not a living thing other than the island's scurrying lizards and crabs in the sand and stunning cormorants flying overhead. Jan, especially, could spend hours nosing about the beach, picking up shells and inspecting tracks or patterns in the sand or leafy ground that could be this or that insect. She's forever hoping to find a big shell intact, such as a bayliss or a trumpet shell, the kind found in Hawaii that locals blow into. It's a fanciful hope – Jan hasn't found one yet. She gets a little teased by the rest of the family as a consequence, who poke fun at her 'hippie' side.

At around eight, after morning coffee at Oscar's, Jan, Dave and Sophie Griffith once again emerged through the members-only gate of Mackay Marina, dressed in crisp summer outfits, Jan looking glamorous as usual in one of her big sunhats, and rolled the esky down the ramp towards *Honey May*. In a scene that was becoming more and more familiar to Jan and Dave's marina neighbours, Sophie bounded towards the two-storey boat with her tongue flapping out. She leapt onto the deck and wriggled her hindquarters as Dave drew ropes in from the shore and Jan buzzed about packing the kitchen and assisting Dave as he steered *Honey May* out of the marina and beyond the headlands.

This time, Jan and Sophie stayed down on the front

deck as Dave drove the boat up on the flybridge – there was no Bridget or Luke to hoist her up and Sophie always seemed a little happier on the lower deck anyway, as it was calmer and less wet. Jan had her deck chair out and sat in it with her feet firmly on the ground, looking out to the horizon and the islands ahead of them. She dangled a hand down to pat Sophie, who was sitting beside her gaping out at the world ahead. The dog sniffed madly at the air for all those salty smells that were becoming more familiar, but clearly no less exciting, every time she came out on *Honey May*.

They had been motoring along for almost an hour when *Honey May* moved past lovely St Bees and Keswick islands, which were stealing the limelight while their baby cousin Aspatria jutted out of the water, comparatively more like a rock growing trees than a lush paradise.

Dave climbed down the ladder and made his way over to Jan and Sophie. 'Ready for a drive?' Dave asked his wife. 'I'll stay down here, just gotta check on a few things. You'll be right on your own, won't you?'

Jan nodded as Dave bent down to Sophie who was standing now and looking up at him eagerly.

'Wanna check on the engine with me, Tuck?' he said, grabbing her head in both hands and rubbing her ears.

Jan climbed the ladder to the flybridge as Dave started moving about on deck with a very happy Sophie, who was panting and ready for the next onboard activity. Jan sat on the swivel stool to man the boat. She looked at the GPS system as it tracked *Honey May*'s way around Aspatria. She knew that pretty soon she'd see Scawfell across seven nautical miles of ocean and they'd be less than an hour away from mooring for a day of fun.

She peered over to the east of Aspatria to try to make out Hesket Rock, just off Aspatria's shore and only sometimes poking out above sea level. This spot always made her nervous. Dave had drummed into her that this was a danger zone. The water got confused, swirling and boiling as it manoeuvred its way around Hesket, which could only be seen at low tide. 'Lots of boats come to grief here,' Dave had told her. It was directly on the route northeast, straight out of Mackay to Scawfell. Dave knew to put a waypoint on the GPS so that *Honey May* steered at least one kilometre around the rock to avoid the water's most tormented patch. Still, it was always a wobbly part of the trip and Jan readied herself.

Down on the main deck, Dave pulled at ropes and moved in and out of the saloon as a contented Sophie followed him around, standing patiently in wait as he fiddled and tweaked, wagging her tail every few seconds. She had all the time in the world. Dave went over to the engine compartment at the bottom of the ladder to the flybridge, opened it up and crouched down, his head under the floorboards. Sophie placed herself beside him, snout raised. She sniffed the warm air, then the briny-oily-smelling space beneath the floor, then Dave's legs and feet, her nose occasionally tickling him as he made sure everything was in working order.

Overhead, though, things were changing – and not for the better. Jan was watching the light of the day dimming as clouds moved in. She noticed that the number of white caps – the frothy borders of waves – was increasing on the horizon. As Aspatria got closer and St Bees and Keswick farther and farther in their rear vision, Jan slowed the boat as Dave had instructed her to do near Hesket. She switched the steering from autopilot to manual so she was able to navigate through the passage herself, moving the wheel as if she were driving a car. She could feel the swivel of the wheel a touch stronger in her hands, adding a string of tension to her control.

The sound of the engine always got a little louder when moving through this narrow passage, as it seemed to ricochet between the boat and Aspatria's rocky caverns. Though *Honey May* was moving quite calmly, the bow began to bounce. The ripples of the ocean turned into mini waves that splashed the clear plastic sheeting over the flybridge. The growl of the boat's wake grew louder as the engine worked a little harder to pull through the swirl. The boat was fishtailing ever so slightly. The wheel felt a little heavier than Jan was comfortable with. The clouds were looming even more than they had just moments ago, and looking a bit ominous.

'Dave,' she called down the steps. Dave continued his fiddling while Sophie's ears pricked at the sound of Jan's voice. 'I think you might need to help me up here.'

'One minute,' said Dave. He glanced up at Sophie

who was looking at him inquisitively, as if to say, *Yes, Dave? What are we going to do now?*

'Tuck, you stay here, girl. I'll just be a minute,' Dave said, stroking her under the chin and soliciting a happy grunt. The pup's head was tilted as he made his way up to Jan on the flybridge level.

Dave toggled switches, pressed a button or two and looked out at the water. He hurried back down to Sophie who was standing at the foot of the stairs, panting and looking up with eager eyes. While they didn't like to pander to Sophie's neediness – the Griffiths' creed being that dogs weren't babies and that they needed their independence – they hated to be apart from her as much as she hated to be apart from them.

On this October morning, Dave realised he had one more adjustment to make and so he climbed the stairs again. 'Stay there, Tuck,' he said and walked across the deck of the flybridge to the steering wheel, leaving Sophie just at the bottom of the ladder. Dave made sure that everything was in manual and Jan was comfortable with the direction. The sun had given way to an overcast day that the weather report hadn't predicted. The wind had come up and there seemed to be a few more ripples in the water beneath them, but *Honey May* was still running smoothly.

Dave gave Jan a rub on the shoulder, saying, 'You right?' Jan nodded her head in the affirmative. After a few minutes spent making sure Jan was comfortable, Dave went back down the steps to the ever-waiting

Sophie. She wasn't directly at the bottom of the ladder where he'd told her to stay. As Dave climbed down, he wondered why she hadn't trotted over to greet him.

'Tuck. Tucker,' he called when he still didn't see her. He waited a minute.

'Tuck. Sophie.' His heart quickened. When no happy pup came bounding, Dave swore. There were not many places to hide on the boat and it wasn't Sophie's way to be difficult. He ran downstairs into the bedroom. He made his way along the side rails to the front deck where Sophie had spent so much time with Jan and Bridget. He saw that she wasn't there either.

In that instant, with a terrible sick certainty, he knew that she was gone. Time stood still.

But not for long.

'Jan! Hit the man-overboard button!' he yelled.

'What? What's happened?' Jan yelled, scrambling for the button.

Dave knew that those first few seconds would be vital if they were to stand any chance of spotting Sophie. Fighting his rising panic, he kept it together as he leant over the rails, making his way all over to see if she was just over the edge. 'Sophie's gone. She's gotta be around though,' Dave yelled out. The boat came to an eerie stop as Jan and Dave began to scream her name. Jan could feel her heart pound. *Was this really happening?*

Fighting his rising panic, Dave raced inside for the

binoculars. It wasn't even mid-morning but the day had become really overcast and the sky was now closer to the grey of Sophie's fur than it was to the sparkly, sultry days Queensland is famous for.

Dave scanned the water and Jan scrambled down-stairs. She was telling herself that all the time Sophie had spent in the water with the family would mean she'd be able to swim. She'd be OK. But the weather was turning against them. 'It was grey, it had become not a nice day and so even if she'd been close, we couldn't have seen her little head,' Jan explains.

Jan took the binoculars from Dave, who hurried up to the flybridge. They decided he would drive the boat back and forth and survey from up there, and Jan would scan from down on the deck.

When their binoculars and yelling yielded no swim-ming pup, Jan's panic really set in. *How could she have disappeared so quickly? What if Sophie had hit the side of the boat? She could have hit the foam and swallowed a mouthful and drowned. The tides could slam her into rocks, knocking her unconscious or worse. Another boat could easily miss her, running her over. Worse yet, the* Honey May *could miss her and run her over.*

The Griffiths drove around, zigzagging and retracing the path back towards Hesket and Aspatria. Maybe Sophie was treading water in the spot she went over-board. The sky darkened even more and the day cooled as they called Sophie's name. The water was so sloppy that it was hard for Jan to keep her balance and focus the binoculars. She began to see things – every white cap became Sophie; every jumping fish or wrinkle in the horizon her sweet dog. She was desperate to catch just a glimpse of those perky blue-grey ears. But with every minute that passed, Jan knew the odds they were playing against were worsening. If Sophie was alive, if she was out there swimming, there were so many natural forces to contend with. *What if she really had hit her head but was still alive, thrashing about out in there? What must she be feeling? Terror. She must be so confused. She would be expecting them to come and scoop her up and wondering why on earth she was out there alone. Could she see* Honey May *and see Jan and Dave yelling over the sides? What if she was watching them, trying to call out but unable to bark. Was she keeping her head above the water?*

Dave was peering across the ocean and imagining Sophie all alone out there. *How could the girl possibly survive? It was water forever.* He had looked out to sea so many times, from his board as a surfer and from *Honey May* as a boat owner, and felt such a sense of fulfilment and peace. He loved the vastness and the energy. But he knew the potential for disaster and since learning more about boating, he was even more aware of it. The idea of Bridget or Ellen swimming out there on their own, injured and terrified, was too much for him to handle; and Sophie was so much more vulnerable. She had no concept of tides or sharks. She had no concept of being alone in the world. And it was he who was responsible.

The guilt set in instantly for both of them. Jan was

loathing herself. *Why had she called Dave up to the flybridge? Why had they left Sophie alone? They never did, ever ever, and now she was out there somewhere. She hated to be away from them. How could they have been so stupid?*

Jan and Dave were thinking all of this and yet saying none of it. They were in emergency mode and their mission was to find Sophie. Their silence was imperative: speak and all their fears would become real.

Dave was alternating between searching and driving, rushing up the ladder to drive *Honey May* forward and anchor her again so they could stop and thoroughly search the area without the noise of the engine interfering with a chance bark or howl. They stopped for ten minute intervals, edging their way around the north side of Aspatria, then getting as close to Hesket Rock as they safely could. They stopped and again yelled Sophie's name over and over.

'Sophie! Sophie Tucker! Here girl! Tuck! Where are you Sophie? Tucker!' They listened and they squinted and they hung themselves over *Honey May*'s railings. They knew every minute that passed was likely to sweep Sophie further from them. They didn't know where she went overboard, exactly, but they'd let her out of their sight for fewer than ten minutes, which in boating talk is equal to far longer. The tide had been high at around half past eight, about ninety minutes before they lost Sophie. This meant that it was gearing up for its peak speed in the next hour and a half. The tide was sweeping north past Scawfell and beyond all the islands.

Why couldn't they see her? How long could she swim out there and why was she not swimming right alongside Honey May, *looking up at them with those gorgeous, trusting eyes, just ready to leap back onboard the tender? She was a strong swimmer but how could she possibly cope with the tides out there that were fierce enough to make* Honey May *rock and to make Jan throw up? Or what if she was swept over coral and sliced like a razor blade? What if she was bleeding? There were sharks that could take one chunk out of her and she'd be a goner – even if there were no sharks to find her, she could bleed to death very quickly. Oh, why couldn't they see her? Why couldn't they see her?*

As the Griffiths searched and motored, anchored and searched and hollered, their energy went from methodical to frenzied and back to matter-of-fact. Dave was going through all the tide information in his head as he yelled, 'Tuck!' and ran back and forth to the GPS system to track as accurate a path as they could. They tried to stay focused as they drove around; they would not give up.

Jan focused her binoculars over to Aspatria, which was about three nautical miles away. She could just see the shoreline, the ripples of waves lapping up and off it. In the now overcast tone of the day, the island looked threatening. It did not look like a place of tropical refuge but a rocky, remote landmass amid a terrible ocean that was so far from their family home and so far from where Sophie had always been safe. Jan looked out into the water and felt ill. This ocean that she had grown up alongside, that had represented so much of the good life that they had worked towards, now seemed to have claimed an irreplaceable part of their lives. Jan couldn't imagine seeing a pup on shore and as the time passed, she could not and did not want to imagine Sophie swimming alone in the water. She was so little and the ocean so eternal.

Experienced seamen will tell anyone chartering a boat that if someone goes overboard, you never take your eyes off them or you'll never find them. 'You've got no hope,' says a friend of the Griffiths, Warren Hill, a skipper, diver and all round seaman who has been making his living from the ocean since 1973. 'If your dog goes overboard, you're not going to hear them bark, are you? Unless you see it happen, they're gone.'

The longer they looked, the more they'd boated miles off course, out into the Coral Sea where the islands disappeared and there was only deep blue and sky all the way to the horizon. When they were hoarse from shouting Sophie's name, the Griffiths had to accept that they'd done as much as they could.

Jan and Dave couldn't look at each other. They'd been circling for two hours, looking and shouting for Sophie. They wanted to give her every chance. But they were also in shock and could think nothing but the worst: no matter how long they looked, Sophie was not going to survive out there. They couldn't admit it to each other but they knew what the other was thinking. It was time to keep moving. The decision was intensely painful but they were too upset to achieve anything further if they kept looking.

Dave's instinct was to go home. How were they going to moor out at Scawfell and mingle in paradise with their friends, knowing that their darling Sophie was lost? 'I just didn't see that there was any hope: she was gone,' Dave recalls. They had circled the area and called out her name. But she was a dog and had gone overboard and there was no sign of her. This was the ocean, and about as far and deep out into it as they could have taken her.

Jan's instinct was the opposite: how could they go home with no dog? Jan's rationale won out. They continued on their planned course. Jan had one bit of hope left: *Maybe, just maybe, we'll come across Sophie along the way or tomorrow when we're on our way home. Maybe she'll somehow know where we're headed – she's been with us to Scawfell, and make her way there. Or maybe, by some miracle, she'll have made it to Aspatria, not so far from where we lost her.* Jan wasn't ready to accept defeat. It just didn't feel right or real; it was only that morning that Sophie was sniffing and trotting about behind first her, and then Dave, the three of them on a leisurely weekend away. Now, Sophie was gone, just like that, it seemed, and they were helpless to find her. *How could she just disappear?* She had to be out there. Jan's maternal instinct was keeping her hope alive even though her heart was aching. It was very likely that Sophie was dead.

The assumption was so strong, the shame so stunning, that Jan and Dave did not discuss the possibility of alerting the authorities. Search parties would have been in place were Sophie a person. It would generally take three to five days for rescue workers to conclude that someone was unlikely to be found alive, and a week for them to call off searches altogether. It took Jan and Dave several hours of very quickly dwindling hope to decide that their 22-kilo dog, so much smaller and more vulnerable than a person, was most likely gone. Drowned. Aspatria was over three nautical miles away, St Bees another half a mile. The tides were turning rapidly and Dave knew from his research that the highest tides on the east coast of Australia were near Mackay. The best thought Jan had was that she had taken a gulp of water and quickly passed out – that she was barely aware. There were too many worst-case scenarios for the two of them to bear.

In the predator-infested waters of the Great Barrier Reef, Jan and Dave knew there were many fates worse than drowning. It was in these waters that famed crocodile hunter Steve Irwin met his end in 2006, pierced in the heart by a ray he'd come too close to. If stingrays could kill a burly man who handled crocodiles for a living, imagine the damage to Sophie. It would only take a scratch or a bite from any number of marine creatures to weaken her and to send the scent of her blood leaking out through the reef.

There were also lethal sea snakes, giant manta rays,

sponges encased in glass crystals that could cause poisonous lesions, fire hydroids that looked like plants and stung like wasps, and so many types of jellyfish, including the box jellyfish that could kill a human in minutes. Not to mention the sharks. Although there were nets and drumlines – baited drums that were less risky than nets to marine life and were attached by one line to the seafloor, another line to a shark hook – all through the Reef in an effort to keep beaches more people- than shark-friendly, there were many sharks enjoying life in the Reef. Whale sharks preferred plankton to flesh, but one nip from any sort of shark tooth was enough to have a dramatic impact on a 22-kilo pup. Hammerhead and tiger sharks, one, two, even three metres long, had been known to take a bite out of anything fleshy they encountered, whether they were going in for the kill or a quick chew.

The thought of Sophie's little legs and her cuddly body dangling under the water for every curious or hungry shark or fish was too grisly for Jan and Dave to contemplate.

In fact, there was much that Jan and Dave were not able to contemplate. They had switched into action mode the minute they discovered Sophie missing, but now they were being overtaken by shock. They had conflicting instincts – conflicting between each other as well as within themselves. Neither of them could quite believe Sophie had gone overboard and neither could imagine exactly how she disappeared so instantly. The reality that she was gone was far from sunken in, but it also seemed preposterous for them to imagine that she was anything but gone. Already, her absence was palpable because ordinarily, she was always around. She should have been there as they eventually continued to Scawfell. She should have been following them, looking up at them, asking with her eyes, *What now? What's happening? Where are we going?*

How she had gone overboard was another question. She might have been flung over the railing as *Honey May* rocked through the passage and hit a swell. Then again, while it was choppy and the boat was certainly not just cruising lightly, Sophie had travelled through this passage many times before without problems. She'd travelled through here just weeks ago on that amazing fishing trip. She had never gone near the sides and they'd never had anything close to an accident with her. She was almost always trailing right alongside one of the family or was down below, lying in the doorway of the kitchen when the sun was getting too much for her or when Dave had decided that there was just too much activity and commanded Sophie to get out of the way.

Jan and Dave only really had one explanation for themselves: Sophie had tried to get up the ladder to the flybridge. They'd left her alone and she'd panicked and tried to get up to them. After all, she'd been up there before. In her urgency, she may have forgotten her consistent reluctance to mount the ladder on her own. Perhaps she'd attempted the climb, slipped and toppled overboard. Or perhaps she'd come around to the side and tried to leap, hit the side and been flung into the ocean. Jan and Dave imagined that she'd made some sort of attempt to get back on the boat, but must have been swept away before they noticed she had fallen. The more they tried to piece together the sequence of events, the more they were forced back to the one indisputable fact: Sophie was gone. She had been a constant companion. She was their buddy and their family. What would they do without her?

It took them less than an hour to get to Scawfell after abandoning the search, by which time it was early afternoon and the sun had come back out. The island was looking as dreamlike as ever, the turquoise water of the bay welcoming the Griffiths to yet another pocket of tropical paradise, the granite rock-bed of the island red and dramatic against the ocean. But Jan and Dave weren't in paradise, they were numb. Neither was talking to the other as Dave moored, unleashing the anchor and throwing ropes overboard in dazed silence.

Ordinarily, mooring was an energetic and bustling affair, with Dave calling out to Jan to unwind this rope and throw that rope precisely 'now'. On that evening, as leisure boats pulled up around them, Jan and Dave were doing all they could not to break down completely. For Dave, this meant focusing on securing the boat and getting on with the night. He worked alone, while Jan, biting her lips and struggling to breathe calmly, opened and shut cupboards in the kitchen trying to prepare something. *But what? Nibbles? Wine? Dinner? How could they eat?* Jan could barely function. She was hoping that their friends would show up and distract them, but she also wanted to crawl into a dark space and go to sleep.

'Eating dinner that night was like chewing on razor blades,' Jan says. The only saving grace was that Ian and Denise did turn up with another couple of friends. The three couples gathered on one of the boats and sat around eating and drinking. Denise and Ian were glowing from their day participating in a Mackay Game Fishing Club competition in which the two of them took a whole lot of wins, including Champion Boat. Denise talked modestly of not only winning the individual competition but of beating Ian – apparently her fiercest competitor – by one Spanish mackerel.

Jan and Dave were doing everything in their power to avoid facing what they were both now thinking was inevitable: that they had lost Sophie and it was their fault. Whether she was out there swimming, which they couldn't quite allow themselves to give up on, or she had drowned instantly, they had let her down and the shock of it all was too much. And they just couldn't bring themselves to tell their friends. Jan feared that if she mentioned Sophie at all, she'd break down completely. She didn't want to do that to them and she couldn't face the grief herself. Jan and Dave did not want to admit what had happened. It was too awful. 'We just felt so bad that we'd let her down. She trusted us so deeply. How could we have been so stupid?' says

Jan now, a quiver still lacing her words. Even now, recalling the day they lost Sophie can be too much, causing Jan to close her eyes or simply change the subject.

So Jan and Dave sat there and tried to participate in the socialising. Boats anchored, deck chairs unfolded, the couples fired up a barbecue and opened bottles of wine, and talk of the day was accompanied by the sound of fish sizzling.

At some point, not long after they'd got settled and as the sun was going down, a boat moored close to them. Jan was staring out to the island, unable to stop scanning the shoreline for signs of Sophie. She noticed that these people had dogs and began to watch with interest as they piled into their dinghy at the back of the boat to motor into Scawfell.

'One was a blue cattle dog,' Jan says. She went to stand up from her folding chair but stopped herself. She looked over at Dave who was leaning on the rail, trying to show interest in the conversation around him. Jan put her arm out and nudged Dave on the shoulder, then nodded her head to the family in the tender. She didn't say anything but Dave knew what his wife was thinking. *Someone could have picked her up!*

'I was being silly but I started to become quite convinced that these people had rescued her,' says Jan. 'I figured they were never going to "fess up". If anyone did find her, they were going to want to keep such a lovely dog.'

The dog wasn't Sophie. It wasn't looking around for Jan and Dave and it wasn't showing any sign of anxiety or exhaustion. There's no way Sophie would have been so calmly hanging with another family, whether she'd just fallen overboard or not. Sophie didn't run away or befriend other people – she was a sociable dog as long as her family was in sight.

Jan watched the family pull their dinghy up on shore and her heart ached.

She sat, quietly nodding at her friends' stories, faking a half smile and barely able to contribute in her usual animated manner. It was an idyllic scene – three couples relaxing over wine and seafood amid the hoop pine trees and azure waters of tropical Queensland, with few worries but what time they might make their way home the next day. But underneath the small talk, there was dread, and by the time everyone else was tucked in for a good night's sleep, Jan and Dave knew their sleepless nights were just beginning.

On the Sunday morning after Sophie disappeared, with the sunrise over Scawfell Island marking almost a day since Sophie had vanished from the Griffiths' lives, Jan and Dave, sleep deprived and in shock, began the long journey back to Mackay. It was ten in the morning and they well knew that this would be the longest twenty-five nautical miles of their boating lives. What had begun as a social and leisurely weekend cruise, the sort that young couples give up busy, urban lives to move to the Queensland tropics for, had already become a sickening memory.

They decided they would follow what they ordinarily referred to as the scenic route back to Mackay, circle Hesket Rock and Aspatria then head towards St Bees and take the Egremont Passage, and hope for any chance, miraculous as it had to be, of spotting Sophie. The mood between husband and wife was fragile. Neither of them spoke much but to plan the day, and to avoid the obvious trauma Sophie's name was not uttered. When Dave spoke, it was to convey distances and directions. They considered the proximity of St Bees Island to where they had lost her, and Dave realised that if they were to keep any hope up, they had to see if she might have made it ashore one of those islands.

He was more than sceptical. His heart was broken, and he thought there was no way Sophie could be out there. This route was, more than anything, to gain some sense of control over a situation that threatened to pull him to bits.

Jan responded to his suggestions by nodding and managing a quarter smile. Her breathing was strained, her hands shaky. Both of them tried to muster a flicker of optimism – *could this really still be put right?* – and they did their best to put on a brave face for each other.

'I was just trying to get the picture of her being hit by the wake of the boat out of my head,' says Jan. 'I had this horrifying image of her beautiful blue coat floating in the water.'

Dave drove the boat while Jan sat beside him, binoculars in hand. Dave, with one hand on his right thigh and the other on the steering wheel in a gesture that made him look far calmer than he actually was, squinted through his prescription sunglasses, hoping for any sign of their girl bobbing out there on the water. It was, no question, a long shot, especially after their effort yesterday. If they hadn't been able to see her just minutes after she'd disappeared, what hope was there after a day and a night of tides? But she was a strong dog, she'd been swimming in the ocean all of her young life and she was a cattle dog with energy to burn. Jan and Dave wanted to imagine that Sophie had swum through the night and would be out there waiting to be picked up.

It would have been terrifying for even the strongest human swimmer, let alone their pampered, adoring Sophie. The idea of her out there alone was so painful. As the day passed, she must have given up on the hope of Jan and Dave coming to rescue her. She would have had to keep moving or she would have sunk. They imagined their treasured dog, only her head poking above the water, jaws clamped, swimming and swimming, moving her legs but not knowing where she was going. Even if she had managed to keep moving, they were horrified by the thought of how scared she'd have been when all the familiar noises of the day – the whirr of boats in the distance, planes and helicopters overhead – gave way to the quiet of the ocean and the sounds of the night. They could only imagine what it must have been like, with the chill of the world going to sleep around her.

They headed towards Aspatria. The expanse of sea separating it from Scawfell looked a little smaller today and Aspatria was a pimple in proportion to Scawfell. Dark rock, thick trees and lots of prickly scrub were all that was visible through binoculars. Dave drove *Honey May* back through the choppy channel that on that day was so much calmer and clearer. Jan wondered, *Had yesterday's conditions been like today's, would they still have their girl? Would their world still be intact?*

There was barely a cloud above them and the water was friendly. The couple took turns on the binoculars, focussing in on Hesket Rock and over to the shore of Aspatria. *Could Sophie have washed up on the island?* Both of them knew it was doubtful but they had to believe enough to try to find her. The sun, however, was powerful, and obscured much of what they might have been able to see. There were glassy reflections on the ocean where yesterday there were white caps. They could see the rocky shore of Aspatria, boulders covered in oyster shells jutting out over small patches of sand. They could see all sorts of sharp debris such as thorny ferns and grasses blown across the shore – and that there was barely a ripple lapping the water up onto the shore, gentle as the day was. All Dave knew was that there was no sign of a tired puppy anywhere out there. There was no Sophie flopped out and waiting for them on Hesket Rock or treading water just off the Aspatria shoreline.

'It was just awful,' recalls Jan. 'I couldn't stop hating

myself for letting her down. I was struggling terribly with the fact that we were going home without her.'

They moved around St Bees and down the Egremont passage. At some point, as *Honey May* veered south, leaving in her wake St Bees and Keswick and moving back towards the coal ships that were lined like soldiers off the shoreline of Mackay, Dave, who was standing on the flybridge, picked up his mobile phone and dialled Luke. Jan was down on the main deck, clutching onto the rail at the bow of the boat, staring in a daze out towards the Mackay Marina that she just did not want to reach. The closer they got the more real it all became. Were they to reach Mackay with no Sophie, they could no longer deny that she was gone. If she hadn't known it was fruitless, Jan might have insisted that they just keep circling around, visiting every island within a hundred-kilometre radius until they had rescued their girl.

Back in Mackay, Luke was at the annual cultural festival, the Mackay Eisteddfod, watching his girlfriend Heather who was doing Scottish dancing. His phone buzzed in his pocket and Luke saw that his dad was calling. He stepped out of the crowd.

'I need you to go to the house,' Dave started the conversation.

Luke put his hand over his left ear to block out the music and said, 'What's going on?'

'Mate, there's been an accident,' said Dave.

Luke's mouth went dry.

'I thought, *Mum's fallen over*. When a parent says something like that to you, you think the worst!'

'Sophie's gone. She fell overboard. We can't understand how, but she did,' Dave said.

Luke's stomach knotted. His ordinarily stoic father was having trouble getting his words out. This had to be bad.

Dave explained as best he could, matter-of-fact but tripping mid-sentence, that they'd lost Sophie and he did not want to talk too much about it – she was gone, they'd looked for her, they were looking again now but were running out of any last remaining hope.

'Can you clean up all of Sophie's stuff so that your mother – so that we – don't have to see it when we get home?' Dave asked Luke.

Dave asked Luke to remove Sophie's water bowl, her food, her lead. He asked Luke to scout around for all her tennis balls and put them in a place where they did not have to see them when they came through the gate, with no weary Sophie riding along in the car with them, no Sophie wagging her tail in delight at being back home.

Dave told Luke, 'I don't care what you do with them, just get rid of them.'

Luke felt sick. 'She's a member of the family,' he says now. 'It was all pretty horrible to take in.'

The only thing to do was jump into action. He drove to the house. The first thing Luke saw as he drove through the remote-controlled wooden gate was the squeaky pork chop, Sophie's favourite toy. 'It would have been like coming home to someone's hat lying around when they've only just gone,' Luke says.

He worked quickly, gathering chewed tennis balls from beneath bushes and fishing a few out of the swimming pool. He took the water and the food bowls and the lead that Dave used to take Sophie walking every day and he threw them in the storage room outside the laundry, down under the house. Luke did the most thorough job he could, knowing that the lump in his throat was nothing compared with what his mum and dad were going through as they made their way back to Mackay.

6

Something Awful Happened

There are many ways to handle grief and Jan and Dave were getting plenty of experience in it. Their initial instinct was to avoid speaking about what had happened, even to one another, and to move on. Their beloved Sophie was gone, but she was a dog, not a person. They hadn't lost a daughter overboard, though the pain was still excruciating. But they had to behave differently to the way they would have done had it been Bridget or Ellen (and this horrifying thought haunted both of them) who toppled over the edge that day.

The Griffiths believed that the bonds between pets and their humans ran incredibly deep. Still, there was only so much room in everyday socialising for the mourning of a cat or a dog. A week might be the limit for how long people can stomach discussions about how much someone misses their Greypuss or Oscar. Jan and Dave had both adored Sophie with a deep, true love, but they still felt that a sense of proportion needed to be maintained. In theory, at any rate.

In practice, the aftermath of Sophie's disappearance was a nightmare for both of them. It was a Saturday in October when Sophie went overboard. Jan and Dave are able to talk about it now but both of them clip the essential details – what time it was when they hit the man-overboard button, how many days it took to tell people. Their vagueness is partly due to the normal strains of time on memory, but mostly to the total trauma, one that forced them to shut out painful details. Jan cried that night at Scawfell – agonising crying with choking and gasping and wailing, as Dave hugged her and said nothing; there was nothing, really, to say.

They can't remember driving through the gate the Sunday evening after she disappeared. They don't want to remember what it was like to return to the house with no Sophie. Dave and Jan weren't talking to each other and were trying not to think to themselves. Jan sat in the passenger seat of the car staring straight ahead. Imagining life without Sophie was inconceivable and it was all too easy to imagine the kind of terror they had allowed their girl to fall prey to. It was best to switch off. They needed to if they were going to survive the ordeal.

They unpacked the car, mechanically putting the

picnic basket back in its closet upstairs and the leftover food in the fridge. They showered and went about getting themselves ready to try to sleep. But another dread was looming: first, they needed to call the kids. They always did when they came home from a jaunt on the boat. The conversations were usually short, as they all came home – Jan, Dave, and Sophie – wonderfully exhausted from the sun and the activity.

Neither Jan nor Dave wanted to break the news. They didn't want to upset the kids, nor did they want to talk about Sophie. But if they didn't call, the kids would worry.

Jan phoned Matthew, left an artificially cheerful message when he didn't pick up, and then called Ellen. 'Mum called and told me point blank,' says Ellen. 'I remember it so well.' Ellen's fiancé, Ben, was on his mobile to his parents and turned around to see Ellen clutching the phone and crying. 'I was trying to keep it together because I could hear how upset Mum was,' remembers Ellen. 'And trying to signal to Ben to reassure him that I was OK at the same time. I remember wanting to know all the hows and whys but I couldn't bring myself to ask. I got off the phone and cried and cried.'

Then Jan dialled Bridget's number. 'Hi, just callin' to say we're home,' Jan said.

'How was it? How's my girl?' Bridget said, immediately. 'Dead from all that swimming?' It was just a figure of speech because Bridget knew that all three of them were always worn out after a trip on the boat.

But the line went silent.

'Everything is fine. Look, I'm too tired to talk.' And Jan put the phone down.

Bridget was left with a silent line and a haunted feeling. What was that all about?

Then her phone rang again.

'What's going on?' asked Bridget. It was Dave on the line. 'Where's Mum?'

'She's gone to bed, she couldn't talk. Listen, we have some bad news,' said Dave. Bridget's stomach dropped.

'What? What is it Dad – tell me!'

'We lost Sophie. She went overboard. Your mother is beside herself. We looked for her but she's bloody gone.'

Bridget can't remember what else was said. She put the phone down and went to bed sobbing. She stayed there for two days. When she slept, she dreamt of Sophie – dark, terrible dreams in which Sophie's legs were moving and moving in the ocean until they couldn't move anymore. She would wake thinking that it couldn't be true. She remembered Sophie on the boat, how happy she always was, how eager and well-behaved and content to just follow her family around. In Bridget's mind, Sophie was still alive. She wasn't close enough to the events to really digest the information her father had given her, with the same note in his always perfectly level voice that had alarmed Luke. Sophie had to be at home, where she was when Bridget left her, taking care of Jan and Dave.

The next day was a blur for Jan and Dave. They had

got home late on Sunday evening and were feeling morbidly shut down, not wanting to deal with anything. Jan wanted to go to bed and sleep for days. Dave wanted to drink a lot of Coronas, not that they did anything for him. In fact, he drank less than he might otherwise have in stressful times because he did not want to get emotional. Both of them wanted to close the curtains, sit at the kitchen table and wait for the phone to ring with a yachtie on the end of the line saying, 'We found your Sophie.'

On Monday morning it was terrible to wake up and realise, all over again, that she had gone and wasn't coming back. Dave had barely slept and when he did open his eyes, there was no Sophie looking patiently at him. There was no Sophie to lick his face. Jan tried to keep sleeping, tried not to open her eyes so it wouldn't be so obvious that Sophie wasn't jumping on her and nosing her face. Sophie had been the first lovely interaction of every morning since Bridget had left home, and she'd made waking up every day a joy. Now the house felt cavernously empty and dreadfully quiet. Both of them had to go to work and yet neither of them felt they had anything to get up for.

They agreed that they couldn't shut down and that going about their day might help distract them.

'We can't let this bury us, love,' Dave said. 'Let's go to Oscar's.'

Around nine, Jan and Dave entered Oscar's as usual for breakfast, determined to get on with life but heavy with grief. Everything was normal there, just as it had been before they lost Sophie. They greeted John, who was steaming milk behind the machine, and Desley, who was sitting at her usual table doing the crossword in the *Daily Mercury*. They sat down, ordered, and looked at each other. The usual conversation – Dave's jobs for the day, Jan's chat with one of the kids that morning (Griffith family catch-up calls started as early as the day breaks in Mackay) – did not begin. All they could discuss was what to have for breakfast and what Jan should pick up for dinner.

Jan was smiling and polite and said, 'Thank you, darling' to the pretty German waitress delivering her skinny latte. When Desley joined them at their table, Jan forced herself to ask how her weekend was. Desley talked about the movie she'd been to see on Saturday night and then wondered right back, how was Jan and Dave's weekend? Dave looked at Jan. *I'll leave this to you.*

'Well,' Jan said, her eyes on her coffee. 'We went out to Scawfell on the boat.'

'Oh. lovely,' Desley said, frowning slightly. She could sense that something was wrong, but perhaps Jan and Dave were just weary, as they often were after their adventures on the boat. 'Was it fishing weather again?'

'Mmm, yep,' Jan said and raised her eyes to Desley's. 'Well, no. We met up with our friends Ian and Denise. They were in a fishing competition.'

Then there was silence. Jan couldn't stand it.

'Actually, Desley,' Jan's voice cracked, 'something awful happened.'

Desley looked at Dave, who just shook his head.

'Oh. Are you OK?' Desley felt awkward and alarmed.

'We lost Sophie,' Jan said and the tears welled up. She wasn't going to cry in public, she couldn't.

'Jan, oh my God,' Desley gasped, putting down the spoon she'd been fiddling with.

'She fell overboard. We were over near St Bees and we left her down on the deck. We only left her for ten minutes. I feel so stupid. It was the first time we've ever left her downstairs alone and now she's gone.'

Desley was picturing Sophie, who she'd met over at Jan and Dave's several times, out there in the ocean. 'She is such a lovely dog. Oh. I'm so sorry.'

'I feel sick about it,' said Jan, clasping both of her hands around her latte as if desperate to warm them. 'We looked for her. We looked and we looked and we just never did see her swimming out to an island,' Jan said. Her eyes were full of tears. 'The worst part is that we just don't know what happened to her. One minute she was there and then she was gone.'

Desley went home that day feeling haunted, herself. 'I kept thinking about this little dog swimming and swimming and swimming and getting nowhere,' says Desley. 'It was just so painful even for me to imagine. I knew it must have been tearing them apart. They really depended on that dog, and they adored her.'

After opening up to Desley, Jan and Dave were very

selective about who they told back in Mackay and only told a few people who were part of their everyday lives. 'I didn't tell very many people at all. I just couldn't. I was so ashamed and I didn't want to think about it any more than I already was,' says Jan. She did call Jenko, who she knew would be nonjudgmental and understanding.

Jenko told Jan the only thing that could have comforted her. 'Mrs Griffith, you mustn't think of her swimming round and round in circles. She would have taken a mouthful of water. Dogs, they have no reflex coordination. She would have taken a mouthful and gone immediately,' Jenko couldn't have been more positive. 'It was really awful,' he says. The shake in Jan's voice was worse than when she'd had to call him about putting Jordy.

Jan kept telling herself that people deal with the death of their pets everyday, but the fact was that there was something extra chilling about Sophie's disappearance, because of all the nightmarish questions it raised. Both Jan and Dave were haunted by endless possible scenarios. They told themselves that she was gone and that she went quickly. But they couldn't help wondering, *what if she was out there?* They were flipping between wanting to imagine she was warm and safe somewhere and returning to the reality that, even if she was alive, she couldn't possibly be warm or safe. How would she cope? She was so reliant on them (not to mention, they on her). Jan pictured her washing up on an island, on Aspatria maybe, surrounded by rocks and ocean and dark mountains. There was not a drop of fresh water on Aspatria and barely food for her to scrounge for: crabs and oysters and fish, perhaps, if she could muster the energy and the wherewithal to fish. Jan was haunted by the thought of her making it to an island, looking around to see where her family was, and finding herself alone. She would have been tired, thirsty, hungry and so confused. Jan was seized by an image of Sophie lying on sand, her head on her paws, her eyes desperate, at the end of her tether and wondering, despairingly, where Jan and Dave were.

Amid the dread there was the occasional flash of optimism that only really served to torture them even more. They couldn't avoid these thoughts, though. *Was there any chance at all that she could have made it?* Sophie was strong and she was a good swimmer and she was smart. If she had survived the fall overboard, she was resourceful enough to look around and thoughtful enough to know where she might survive and where she might not. She would look to see where the nearest land was and she would know to head for wherever she could detect human activity. 'She is certainly bloody-minded enough to make a plan,' Jan would think to herself.

But these were just vague thoughts and hopes. Deep down, Jan and Dave both believed that Sophie was gone. They were trying to accept it, but it was hard when there was nothing to hold on to. One minute Sophie was part of their day, the next she was . . . *A memory? They weren't going to be able to say goodbye?* Jan closed her eyes when the disturbing images came into her head. She took deep breaths and tried to conjure peaceful images of Sophie experiencing what people talk about in near-drowning experiences: the light and the silence. No pain, no fear.

One morning during that first week, Jan woke up and felt that she needed to speak with someone other than Dave and the kids about their loss. The shame was getting deeper; Jan was being consumed by the feeling that they'd let Sophie down, that they should never have taken her on the boat and that they'd been terribly negligent.

She decided she'd call her old friend Heather – a decision she would later thank her lucky stars for.

Jan and Heather were part of a small group of women who held sometimes-raucous ladies' luncheons at each other's houses every few months; lunches that often involved a spell in a swimming pool and maybe a hangover or two the next day. Heather, who had been enjoying Sophie's presence at the ladies' luncheons at Jan's place for years, was herself a dog lover with a fluffy white poodle called Carly, who she and her husband, Tommy, took with them on their boat when they sailed around the Whitsundays.

'Jan rang up, in floods of tears, devastated,' recalls Heather. 'She said, "We lost Sophie. Overboard." It was just agonising, I felt for her so much. We both cried.'

Jan needed a comforting voice, some empathy, some easing of the weight clutching at her, the suspicion that she had failed as carer to Sophie. 'I think Jan knew,

because we take our dog out when we sail, that I understood how easy it would be to lose a dog overboard.
And a lot of people wouldn't. People might have been
very cruel about it but I knew that it could happen so
easily. We take Carly out all the time and we wouldn't
have it any other way. She'd be so upset to be left behind,
but it's always a fear in the back of your mind.'

There was not a whole lot to say on the phone but Jan
needed to let it out. She's not an easy crier and it was a
great challenge for her to open up to Heather. 'I just felt
that she needed to know,' says Jan. She did feel a little
better after hanging up. Later, over dinner, Jan told
Dave how understanding Heather had been. 'Accidents
happen on boats and it's impossible to protect a dog
entirely,' was Heather's final take on it.

Dave barely heard what Jan was saying. It was a small
comfort remembering that they weren't the only ones
who took their dog out, but still, he felt rotten. He had
been to work the past few days, trying to keep busy with
jobs, but he wasn't really there. He barely heard what
anyone said to him. He tried to join in the coffee conversations with his men around the shed, but he stood
there, mostly mute. He certainly wasn't joking around
the way he usually would. Being there helped keep his
mind off Sophie, somewhat, but whenever he sat still,
the thought of those horrible hours crept in, of circling
and seeing nothing but grey sky and choppy water.

Dave was having a hard time coming through the
gate when he got home in the afternoons and had to

switch his brain off completely when he went for his evening Corona. No afternoon walks for him anymore. He missed the company of Sophie following him everywhere. He wanted to chat to her and was spending a lot of his days trying to think of nothing in order to avoid thinking about how horribly quiet it was around the house. When he watered the garden, he didn't know whether to whistle to himself or choke up. He and Jan were both suffering and the vibe between them was less breezy as a consequence.

Over the ensuing days, Jan continued to cry whenever she thought of Sophie, which wasn't at all like her. The four Griffith kids shot emails and phone calls back and forth, discussing what they could do to help. Dave, a natural listener, sat back in discussions more often than he had before the awful event that had redefined the Griffiths' lives. And, after the necessary people had been informed, aside from the odd time when someone would ask about the wonderful Sophie, Jan and Dave did not mention her name, even to one another.

7

Sophie –
the Castaway Dog

It was about noon one day in the first week of December 2008, over a month after Sophie had gone overboard. Brian Kinderman was making his way back to the Keswick Island guesthouse from the island's landing strip, where he would greet and farewell every plane coming to and from Keswick. The moustachioed former corporate manager, who moved to Keswick four years ago to start a new life out of the Brisbane rat race, was wearing his usual island attire of denim shorts and slip-on canvas flats, along with a fluorescent-yellow polyester safety vest so that the planes could spot him. The day was hot and glaringly sunny, as they had been for months during this hotter and drier dry season than any of Keswick's few residents could remember, and Brian was motoring in the golf buggy up the dirt road when he came across a dog.

It was a dark-blue dog flecked with chunks of swarthy grey, small pointed ears pricked but for a little flop in its left, and it was standing solid and alert, legs splayed slightly apart, in the middle of the road and staring at Brian.

A dog.

It was a surreal sight. Brian forgot where he was for a second. This wasn't suburban Brisbane, it was a remote island and dogs were forbidden. Brian looked behind him back to the airstrip. *Was there a boat moored down there? Where had this dog appeared from? And why was it stopped, staring at him?*

A week or so earlier Brian's fellow islander, Mike Barnett, said he had seen a dog making its way down his residential road at about five in the morning near the island's one and only roundabout. Mike had told Brian and a few of the others that he'd tried to follow the dog but had lost it near the beach. 'Have another beer,' was the joking response to Mike's sighting.

But here it was. Mike hadn't been imagining it.

They'd all figured if there *was* a dog, it must have come over with yachties who had moored overnight. But now, a week later, Brian realised that this dog might not have a yacht to return to. As he slowed the buggy to a stop, the dog didn't move. It looked skinny and ragged. He could see the dog's ribs and its fur looked wiry and askew. If it had been here for more than a week or so, Brian thought it must be terribly thirsty. There was no fresh water on Keswick and the residents got theirs by collecting rainwater, of which there had been none for months. 'She wasn't looking very good,' he remembers.

The dog stared Brian directly in the eye but intermittently turned its head away, coyly. It seemed to want to engage him but was not making the first move. It wasn't threatening either, though, or noticeably frightened. Brian didn't know if it was inviting him over or trying to show him something. It was tentative but not unfriendly.

'I got out, grabbed the rope from the back of the buggy and tiptoed very gently towards it, saying, "G'day boy, g'day".'

Brian and the dog had a genial Mexican standoff. Brian got close enough to hear it pant. 'It looked as though it was checking me out. It wasn't scared but it wasn't softening either; just stood there like a statue.'

But just as Brian got close enough to hold his hand out, the dog bolted. There was not a split second between its stillness and its bolt. Brian tried the rope as a lasso, whirling it in the air twice and hurling it towards the dog that was, by now, not hanging around. It was already off, galloping up the road towards Keswick's twenty scattered houses.

Brian ran back to the buggy and took off in pursuit, going the island's speed limit of 20 kilometres an hour. In a scene straight out of a *Looney Tunes* cartoon, the dog led Brian up and down hills, never straying from the road. 'It kept looking back at me, as if to say, *are you still following me?* I got the feeling it was taking me somewhere.'

Why Brian was following the dog wasn't exactly clear, even to Brian himself. 'What would I have done if I'd caught it? I would have taken it home with me and at least given it food and water, but I would have to have called the EPA (Environment Protection Agency) because animals other than the natives aren't allowed on the island. We've all said goodbye to some really beloved pets to come here.'

Brian followed the dog as fast as he could, across a quarter of the island, down 'Goat Road', which leads through Keswick's new development plots and to the beach, where Keswick's manicured lawns and tousled gardens of native maiden's blush and macaranga trees give way to scrub and bush.

It was between the bush and the beach at Basil Bay that Brian lost the dog. 'I was following for ages, telling myself I was going to catch up to it. It kept looking around as if to make sure I was still there. Then all of a sudden, it disappeared into the undergrowth. I stopped the buggy and ran into the bushes, but it was gone.' Brian searched and called out, 'Here boy!' for an hour, but to no avail. The mysterious visitor had melted back into the wild.

A visitor to the 530-hectare Keswick Island could laze around for days without seeing anyone. Eighty per cent of the island is wild, tropical land, most of it mountains thick with rainforest foliage, thousand-year-old cycads and grass trees, their fat trunks sprouting long needles of grass. Cessna pilots who fly over the island, usually from Mackay's airport, 34 kilometres away on the mainland, look down to see the sort of undulating wilderness that would have confronted Australia's first settlers. Strewn through the mountains and around the perimeter of the island are thickets of mangrove, swamps overhung with towering paperbark trees, and plots of eucalyptus species including blue gums, poplar gums and bloodwood. Scattered around the island's shoreline are five white-sand beaches, dazzling yet rugged. These beaches mostly go unvisited for days or months at a time. Crabs and hundreds of tiny brown skinks have the run of them, as do the tumbleweeds and driftwood that sweep up and across the sand when winds are high, which is often, as Keswick is in the firing line of the region's prevailing south-easterly winds.

A honeymoon couple staying at the island's one and only guesthouse could sit on the beach of Basil Bay with a bottle of wine and be left alone for hours or days but for the odd nosy crab or a passing goanna. The only human activity that the romancing couple might encounter would be one of Keswick's fourteen (and rising) permanent residents kayaking by, or strolling down one of the island's fire tracks to enjoy their own bottle of wine as the sun streaks pink and orange over the Coral Sea.

The monitor lizards on Keswick are unfazed by predators because, for the most part, there are none. They have to keep an eye out for the sea eagles and crows swooping overhead, but on the ground there are only non-venomous snakes and spiders. There is nothing bigger than the monitors – no goats, no kangaroos, no dingoes, dogs or cats.

Keswick, unlike many of its surrounding islands including St Bees, has been kept free of introduced species, and the residents are prohibited from having pets of any kind. Keswick's tourism campaign calls it 'the last Whitsunday paradise', and proudly references its hundreds of happy bird species and its disease-free Caucasian bee population, a result of hundreds of years of isolation.

The human outpost is on the island's south-eastern side, occupying a crescent of land barely visible from most of Keswick's beaches or even from the dozens of leisure boats that motor by every weekend. Yachts passing through the Egremont Passage or looking across from St Bees might not even spot the tea-green guesthouse, perched like a stork above a steep descent, overgrown with rainforest that drops directly into Horseshoe Bay. The rest of Keswick's houses – lightweight timber constructions painted in muted blues, greys and green that dot the village's gentle hills – are barely visible. There are twenty houses, a building site for four more, a 480-metre airstrip and the refurbished guesthouse owned by Brian Kinderman and his wife, Lyn.

Residents rumble along half a dozen graded dirt roads with names like Azure Bay Drive and Coral Passage Drive in electric golf carts. They spend their evenings on their balconies watching sunsets over the island's rainforest and coral-lined shores and most of them can see far out into the tropical ocean, past the flashy Brampton and Hampton islands all the way up the Great Barrier Reef.

They spend weekends tending to gardens of native species and, in the springtime, they gather for dinner parties at the guesthouse to watch pods of humpback whales moving through the Egremont Passage as they migrate southwards. Jero Andrews, who moved to Keswick in early 2008 and who's spent most of his life around boats and water, has been kept awake all night by the sounds of whales jumping and splashing in the lead-up to mating. Island residents have witnessed whales giving birth as they've sipped their morning cappuccinos. The whales might spend the next few months lingering in Egremont before moving on with babies in tow.

There are no shops or cafés on the island. The biggest intrusion from the civilised world is the Cessna planes dropping off architects and construction workers as well as groceries and cases of wine for the days, weeks, and months ahead.

Keswick visitors, of which there may be three hundred or so a year, can sit and gaze at eagles and sea hawks, snorkel around Basil Bay at high tide with sea turtles and lounging sting rays, or wander from one bay to the next, photographing dramatically-sculpted coral. They can hike along fire tracks and a couple of walking trails, watching tree snakes slide up and over branches or a monitor lizard stand on its hind legs. The only real danger is the island's silver-striped bees that bother no one unless provoked by strong whiffs of perfume.

Brian was really the first person to encounter the dog, and for weeks afterwards he regaled his fellow islanders and guests with full details of the low-speed chase. The thought of the mysterious dog battling to survive out there on the island both haunted and delighted Keswick's inhabitants. Pets and missing them terribly was a common topic of conversation over drinks, as most of the residents had given up some beloved four-legged family member to make their life on the protected island. That's if it wasn't too painful to talk about, as it was for Lyn Kinderman, who found giving up her two cats when she and Brian moved to Keswick so heart-breaking, that she'd need a few glasses of wine to even begin to open up about it. 'We sent them to a cattery. I can't talk about it or I'll cry,' she says.

So when this elusive dog showed itself to Brian in early December it became the talk of the island, as Keswick residents realised that there were now too many sightings for it to be an accidental temporary visitor. Karen Cooke's memory was jogged back to a few weeks before Mike Barnett spotted the dog near the roundabout, when she saw an animal dropping on the Connie Bay walking track, a steep dirt climb that runs approximately three kilometres, from the residential side of Keswick to the shore.

Karen, being a typically vigilant island inhabitant, noticed that the dropping was not like any she had seen from the wildlife on the island, and when she investigated the surrounding bush, she noticed an area of flattened grass. At the time she couldn't imagine what it might have been, but when the dog was sighted first by Mike and then Brian, it seemed likely that she'd seen evidence of a dog camping out.

At nightly gatherings, residents swapped stories and theories about where the dog had come from, where it was now, and how on earth it was surviving. They worried about how it could possibly be finding enough to drink, as it hadn't rained in months. A few of the residents' tanks were even getting low. It was also hotter than the usual low thirties perfect summer temperatures. 'We were all beginning to feel really uneasy. There was no water anywhere and unless the dog was skulking around very quietly, sucking water from pot plants, it must have been suffering terribly,' says Lyn Kinderman.

Beyond water to drink, what was the dog actually eating? No one was noticing that any food was going missing from kitchens or bins. There were birds and lizards out there but enough for a dog to live off? It could have been having a go at the ground-dwelling coucal pheasants or the notoriously dopey curlews, and there were non-poisonous tree snakes that could perhaps provide a meal if the dog was clever enough. It could definitely be fishing along the shoreline but it would want to be careful not to get sliced by coral. Mostly there was not much out there for a lone dog to survive off, and an awful lot of dangerous stuff for it to be wary of.

Resident Eva Browne-Paterson swore she heard barking over several nights, that woke her up feeling distressed and protective. Mike Barnett, who was in charge of keeping an eye on the security of the island, was making an effort to find the dog when he went out on his daily rounds in Keswick's only four-wheel-drive vehicle. He had not seen the dog since his first sighting early in the morning outside their house, but he and his wife Lyn did spot paw prints. They would walk the three and a half kilometre track to Arthur Bay and on several occasions over the course of a week or two, they noticed a trail of paw prints that came out of the rain-forest towards the shoreline and then back again. Mike and Lyn, an avid animal lover who would rescue a caterpillar or an ant from her balcony and take it to the garden, went up close to inspect the trail, recognising them as dog prints. They figured the dog must be coming on to the beach for a swim or maybe to fish.

Despite the huge temptation to be pet owners again, Mike and Lyn knew that even if they'd been able to trap it, the dog would have to go. 'We wouldn't have been able to keep it but we would have tried to find someone in Mackay to take it,' says Mike. Calling the pound or the rangers was not an option. 'They would have destroyed the dog if they couldn't catch it. And it did not seem to want to be caught. They would have had no choice; it's their job.'

All the Keswick residents were looking out for the dog as they went about their daily business. They knew that with every day that passed, the dog's odds were getting worse. If it wasn't dehydration or starvation, it could be the rangers that got to it. Keswick simply wasn't a friendly place for a domestic animal to be.

The only words that are really adequate to describe Sophie's long, lonely sea swim are 'miraculous' and 'unprecedented'. When you get out to the middle of the ocean and look out across the vast distances of treacherous turbulent water she must have covered, it is almost impossible to believe that she made it. But at some point after the morning of 25 October when she went overboard, whether it was twelve hours or twelve days, Sophie scrambled onto the shore of Keswick, which was about five nautical miles from where Dave and Jan hit the man-overboard button on *Honey May*. She was no doubt caked in salt, exhausted and traumatised. Her fur would have been bladed and sticking to her skin, and it's difficult to imagine the extent to which her shoulder and hip joints throbbed from all the swimming she'd done.

She must have been in terrible shock from the

moment she went into the water but her survival instincts compelled her to keep moving – this is the only explanation that vets and dog experts can come up with for how she managed to make it as far as she did. For a dog to spend more than thirty minutes or so in a swimming pool or a lake, even a dog with the greatest affinity for water, would be a muscle-cramping feat. Put the dog in the middle of the ocean, swimming five, six, possibly ten or more nautical miles, competing with tides, currents and the massive influence of the islands and reefs that the ocean bullies its way around – the feat is even more amazing.

'It would take a dog as tough as a cattle dog to do that,' says Australian vet Rob McMahon. 'They are amazingly resilient, bred to work probably one of the toughest jobs a dog can do.'

'I reckon it was virtually physically impossible for the dog to swim to land when you take the adversity of the currents into account,' says Warren Hill, the Griffiths' mate and an experienced seaman. 'There's no way she would have managed it without a lot of help from Mother Nature, in terms of getting lucky with the tides.'

Dogs can be great swimmers. In the droving days, working dogs swam the rivers to herd sheep and cattle. Treading water, however, is a different concept. When dogs swim, they don't let their head go under water and they need to paddle to stay afloat. They are either moving or they're floundering. They also tend to have poor reflex coordination, as Jenko noted to Jan after that terrible

October day, to fend off all the water splashing into their mouths. There are stories of robust working dogs drowning in shallow creeks because they swallow too much water, or being drowned by kangaroos holding their heads down in what could barely be called puddles. So for a dog to survive a long swim in choppy seas, something that would of course tax most humans, really is freakishly unlikely. The strain of keeping from swallowing seawater would have been immense.

The tides were still high but had started going out two hours before the approximate time Sophie went overboard, so they were picking up speed. Tides turn every six hours and twenty-five minutes and are at their fastest three hours after turning, so Sophie went in the water just as the speed was gearing up to its strongest. It would have been moving north away from Mackay, out into the Coral Sea. Unless she was caught up in eddies created by the islands, which might have worked in Sophie's favour and swept her to Aspatria before she was once again caught in the outgoing tide, Sophie would have had no choice but to go with the north-flowing water until the tide slowed down for its change. Only exceptionally strong swimmers can swim against a current, and of course it's impossible to swim against the tide. The best guess is that she'd probably have been out there for at least twelve hours. She had never previously swum for more than ten or fifteen minutes at a time on the Mackay beaches. Her little dog legs must have been unbearably tired.

Jero is a long-time windsurfing practitioner and instructor who paddles on his wave ski around Keswick and St Bees several times a week and finds it mind-blowing that a dog survived to swim the distance that Sophie did. 'I believe that if I fell off my wave ski out there, after half an hour I wouldn't be able to swim any more and would just go where the wind and tide wanted to take me,' he says.

Swimming at night, her visibility would have been seriously challenged. The night of 25 October was close to a new moon, meaning that there would have been virtually no light for her to see the land in front of her, let alone scramble onto shore over all manner of tropical reef hazards. 'If it's night time it's even harder,' says Warren Hill. 'The dog's a land cruiser, how's she going to know which way to go?'

Sophie's heart was in excellent condition from all her beach and next-door-block running, but as fit as she was, she may as well have been a flea in the face of the elements out there. 'Luck,' says Warren. 'She would have had no say in the matter of where she went. She got incredibly lucky.'

Given the likelihood that the wind was south-easterly, it's probable that Sophie drifted north to northwest with the outgoing tide until the next change, around four hours later, when she would have been dragged back south towards St Bees and Keswick. Warren believes that she must have been just bang in the middle of the Egremont Passage when the tides changed, miraculously at just the right spot to be sucked south by the funnel effect of the Passage as it rushes between Keswick and St Bees. Had she been too far from its 'suck factor', she may never have made it to land. And once she was pulled into the Passage, it was something close to divine intervention that took her to shore. 'The current travels northwards all the time and carries the sand and everything else right up to Papua New Guinea,' he says. 'If that dog had missed getting onto one of those islands, it would have died for sure because it would have been swept out into the ocean.'

Seamen can speculate about what happened to Sophie that night but with all the factors at work, only Sophie will ever know. From the spot that Jan and Dave hit the man-overboard button, past Hesket Rock to Keswick, depending on which way around St Bees the tides and currents swept her, the distance is five to seven nautical miles. If she was swept there the night after she went missing, rather than hitting elsewhere first, she'd likely have been swimming for a whole day or possibly longer.

She'd have been able to detect Aspatria, then St Bees, then Keswick as she swam. They might have looked like foreboding blobs to her but they were also carrying the smells of life, and that must have driven her to direct herself, as far as she was able, towards one of them.

It's also possible that she hit Aspatria first, then, realising that she was entirely alone out there and without a drop of fresh water, decided to swim again towards the outline of land that she could see in the distance. She would have been picking up human smells that spurred her on. Perhaps she forced herself to keep going and tackle the kilometre between Aspatria and St Bees. If so, she would have been rewarded with fresh water from one of the island's sixteen natural springs. She might have hit its east coast and traipsed her way through its dense hills or around its treacherous shores to the west coast, facing Keswick.

Why she would have decided to swim again, nobody knows, but swim she did. To reach Keswick, where Mike and then Brian saw her, she would have had to navigate the Egremont Passage, a feat no Keswick resident would attempt, themselves, as the water roars through it with currents as high as five to eight knots and teems with vigorous marine life including sharks. Sophie had somehow survived all the stinging and biting threats out there in the ocean, creatures who needed to take but one nip, swipe or even a brush to destroy her.

Whatever her exact route, it seems that Keswick was the first place that she decided to stay. Karen Cooke's memory is that she saw the dog poo on the path around Connie Bay in the first half of November, so it seems that Sophie hit Keswick early in her ordeal. Perhaps she came ashore on Connie Bay, around three kilometres uphill from the residential development.

The three-year-old pup had survived the almost unsurviveable, achieved a feat that would prove too much for any but the most champion human swimmer.

She was in shock, exhausted, alone. She'd lost her family, to whom she was utterly and single-mindedly devoted, but had somehow made it to this unfamiliar place. Now she had a whole new set of problems.

How could she not have been famished? Even if she had come across a coral trout or a queen fish, the leg of a turtle or some other sort of marine tucker along the way, and had managed to snap at it whilst swimming, she would still have been ravenously hungry, nose sniffing for the scent of anything that might sustain her.

She'd have shaken herself off, as dogs do when they've been swimming. This was no fun paddle she'd been for, though, and Sophie's fur and skin must have been marinated in salt. She must also have been numb with cold. The island's hot spell was fortunate in this sense, even if it meant she was facing a struggle to find drinking water. Sophie could dry herself out as she absorbed her new solitary reality.

She might have barked and wondered, *Could Jan and Dave hear her?* When she looked up from the shore, she'd have seen boulders and cliffs paths leading every which way into the island centre, thick with trees and all sorts of grass and shrubs and foliage. But this terrain that would have had Sophie twitching with excitement had she been accompanied by her family, would now have been terrifying.

Never had she spent more than an evening without Jan and Dave or one of the Griffiths to look after her. She hadn't ever had to think about dinner for herself and she'd never even had to let herself out of the house in the morning for a pee. Sophie was alone, a dog who had gone from pet store window to family life, and all the meaty and air-conditioned treats that came with it. Had Jan and Dave allowed themselves to think about it, they would have wanted to believe that, in the unlikely event that she had made it to land, she would have switched instantly into wild dog mode, surging off into the bush, teeth bared, like a hunter dog. She might have been a pampered pet but the Griffiths had always encouraged her to follow her dog instincts as well. Dogs aren't babies, as Jan would say.

Nevertheless, they wonder now how on earth she coped when she landed on Keswick. *What was the first thing Sophie did after dragging herself ashore? Did she sleep for hours? Did she stand at the edge of the gentle waves looking out to the ocean? Did she whine and whimper? Did she howl? Was she so tired she couldn't move or so scared that she forced herself to a rock or a cave to hide and wait for Dave and Jan? When did all her hope of seeing them fade? How aware of time was she – of how many hours she'd already been deserted and how many more days she was going to be out there?*

Now, washed up on a barely inhabited island with very little meaty wildlife for her to live off – even if she was able to work out how to hunt for her own food – her dog mettle was about to be truly tested. How would her suburban upbringing as a civilised pet and her attachment to the Griffiths fare out here?

With her measured personality and cushy upbringing, she is likely not to have set off on the hunt for food immediately. As with children, a dog's adventurous spirit is often dependent on its sense of security. Without their owners around to offer reassurance, most dogs become anxious in a new environment. In the same way that Sophie tends to take her time to feel completely comfortable around new people, the Griffiths imagine that she would have taken a while to work out where she was. She'd have let time pass to see what came with it. No doubt her already shrinking stomach, which had been lovingly tended to all her life with two meals a day and many snacks in between, would have been gnawing at her, but it's too easy to imagine that she spent hours, even days looking out to sea for a glimpse of *Honey May*. Lying at the shoreline the way she used to lie on the edge of the pool in the sun, waiting for Jan and Dave to come home.

A few days might have gone by before some version of the new reality set in: a reality in which Sophie was an island dog left to fend for herself. She would certainly have swallowed some seawater while she was swimming, which must have made her throw up. She was lucky the dehydration didn't kill her. If she was over on Connie Bay in the early days, as Jero suspects and Karen's sightings suggest, she was in possibly the only part of the island where there was any real chance of finding water. Connie Bay edges a forest of melaleuca trees. Most of the ground in the forest remains damp nearly all year round and even after four hot, dry months, there would have been water below the surface. Sophie could have dug a hole to seep the water out. It would have been brackish – a combination of salt and fresh, which is not ideal for hydration – but it would have kept her alive. 'It's probably the only place I know of with any water on Keswick Island. She definitely landed in the right bay,' says Jero.

By the end of November, Mike Barnett had seen her trotting down his road early in the morning. It's possible that Sophie wanted to get closer to humans. Perhaps she had come into the residential area to look for Jan and Dave when Mike Barnett saw her. She'd probably have been able to hear the sounds of the building site that started up early every morning, with bulldozers and hammering and obscured sounds of male voices. She must have noticed the planes, too, and possibly even discovered the airstrip, near which she had the stand-off with Brian.

By then she was getting skinnier and no doubt thirstier. Incredibly, while these people would have been the solution for her awful hunger, her ravaging thirst and unwanted isolation, it would seem that for Sophie, loyalty was trumping salvation. She might have been terrified and famished, but it would seem that she wasn't about to approach one of these people for help. Sophie had always been friendly with other humans so long as she was with one of the Griffiths, but she was not a dog who lavished her affections on strangers. She was a staunchly one-family dog, and it appears she stayed that way, even when she was fighting for survival. She doesn't seem to have approached the smattering of houses just a brief run away from the beach. As far as anyone can tell, she didn't deign to rummage through bins for fresh scraps and she certainly didn't break down kitchen doors in the middle of the night to get her jaws around the home-cooked food that she must have been able to smell.

All this would later prove endlessly endearing to the Griffiths, who, despite the fact that it pains them terribly to think of their adored pet's suffering, love the fact that, so far as they can tell, Sophie's self-containment and unflagging loyalty extended to her life on the island. Even when she was flung from the lap of luxury to the unfamiliar wild, she seemed to hold out for the owners she loved and formed her strongest attachment to. In her loyal mind, she didn't need to be rescued by the human race, she needed to be rescued by Jan and Dave. And so far, no one was smelling quite like them.

8

Life After Sophie –
One Foot in Front of the Other

Losing Sophie wreaked havoc on everything Jan and Dave had been building their lives towards. Jan had only just started getting her days into gear after Bridget left, and had been coming to terms with the scary but exciting idea that it was only her and Dave from now on, after more than two decades of their children being the heart of everything. Sophie had been there for every high and low moment of the shift. She had allowed them to adjust to a quieter home and pretend that home wasn't entirely an empty nest. Sophie needed them just as much as they needed her.

Now she was gone, in such a shocking way, and Jan was getting nowhere in dealing with it. The fact that Sophie had disappeared out of their care and that they just did not know what their pet had been through would always make recalling the circumstances a more bruising memory than if Sophie had died in some tangible way – a spider bite in the backyard, perhaps. It was sad when Jordy died, as with the death of any pet, but the Griffiths were also suffering from the uncertainty and drama of what had happened.

Dave and Jan gave themselves a mantra: *one foot in front of the other*. They carried on their lives in Mackay seemingly as usual, breakfasting at Oscar's, going to work, having a Corona, but every day was a challenge. Afternoons for Jan were especially terrible. She knew that staying active would help her mood but she didn't have her walking partner and she couldn't bring herself to go on her own, as it would only foreground the awful absence of her buddy. She was once again flung into wondering how to fill the cavernous home that had bustled for so many years with the noise of children and dogs.

She knew that there were a lot of things that she could and should be doing to get on with what could be a very exciting stage of life. In the wake of Sophie's disappearance, though, contemplating anything big was too daunting. When Bridget left home, she'd talked about getting back to the golf she'd played in the early years of her marriage. After Sophie's loss, Jan had brief moments of wondering whether now was the time to just do it: sign up for a few sessions and get out there again. But it was all too overwhelming.

Jan didn't really even have the stomach for cooking,

which was usually one of her great passions. She put food in front of Dave every night but her heart wasn't in it.

'Ellen and I had visions of Mum and Dad sitting on the couch in complete silence. I'm sure we were being overly dramatic but we were so worried about them. Their days revolved around Sophie,' says Bridget.

In fact, the Griffith daughters weren't being neurotic. Jan and Dave were having a hard time at home with each other without the conviviality of Sophie's company. 'For ages we were just lost for conversation because we had no routine anymore,' says Jan. We felt so miserable without her.

Reticence and their own guilt were at work on Jan and Dave throughout the weeks and months following Sophie's disappearance. They felt as though they were carrying around a shameful secret. Their personalities already determined a certain level of stoicism and the very real possibility of criticism from other dog owners in their small hometown threatened to validate their own nagging doubt that they hadn't done the right thing in taking Sophie on the boat. 'I know what Dad would have been thinking,' says Bridget now. 'He didn't say it but I know my dad. He would have been thinking, "I failed her. I had a duty of care, and I failed her".'

All the joyful memories – of her first bound down the marina ramp into Jan's arms on *Honey May*, of every gleeful greeting session just inside the house gate – made her absence hard to bear.

For Dave, as well as Jan, the things that he loved to do

would only slap him with a reminder of the ghastly hole in their lives. For Dave, the boat had always been a source of relaxation and inspiration but how could he go down there now? Staying at home was not much better, though. Dave had no one to follow him around the garden or sniff at the pool filter box. At the weekends he was lost without Sophie sitting beside him when he looked up from the newspaper or decided that it was time for some exercise.

In some ways, talking to Bridget on the phone helped Jan, but in others it exacerbated the pain. Bridget knew that her parents were hurting and she herself didn't want to lose it on the phone. Her first question after, 'How's things?' had always been, 'How's my girl?' For the first few weeks after Sophie's disappearance, mother and daughter had much shorter daily conversations than usual because they both knew they would lose it if they talked about Sophie. Bridget admits that the loss of Sophie injected an unwelcome awkwardness into her interactions with her parents.

When Bridget did come home from university, several weeks after Sophie went overboard, she struggled. She missed Sophie terribly, herself. From the moment she came home, it was obvious how different things were. There was no puppy licking and loving her as she drove through the gate, or sleeping in her bed at night. She couldn't escape the house to sit on the steps with her favourite mate or try to compete with Dave for Sophie's attention.

But Bridget was also spooked by the lack of happy chaos in the house. Things seemed quiet and, well, terribly normal. Her parents were going about their days but there was no mischief in the air, none of Dave's roguish digs or Jan's delight in cooking. When Bridget stood in the kitchen chatting to Jan while dinner bubbled on the stove, Bridget struggled to fill in the gaps when she wasn't telling Jan about which Mackay friend was getting married or not going to university.

For Dave, a few weeks of this lacklustre existence was all that he could stand. He avoided going down to the boat for as long as he could after losing Sophie. The thought of going to clean her up and, eventually, to take her out again when the kids were in town, was initially too much to handle. But there is only so long one can leave a boat to its own devices in the busy Mackay Marina.

Dave started going down to *Honey May*, desperate for distraction. At weekends he would check on the engine, sand and polish and inspect, and say hello to friends down at the marina. The boat gradually became a positive in Dave's days again. The irony was that the more he missed Sophie and the worse he felt about how it had all gone down, the more he was craving being back out on the boat, even just docked. He would go down there in the afternoons to read newspapers or boating manuals, or he would sit and chat to fellow boaters for hours about the weather, the news and planned trips. Being on *Honey May* was therapy for Dave.

Not so for Jan. 'It was unnerving for me,' Jan says of

the idea of going to sit on the treasured boat after Sophie had gone, while Dave fussed around with engine repairs, or sanding and scrubbing walls. 'I was really spooked about going to the boat and just hated the mere thought of hanging out on her.'

The Griffiths had loved to spend a day or a night onboard *Honey May* down at the marina. They didn't need to go anywhere – they liked to relax on her deck and have dinner. It was a holiday without going anywhere. But in the immediate aftermath of the accident, the idea didn't even really come up. Dave and Jan knew between them that the boat was no longer a place of relaxing memories, at least not for Jan, at least not for now.

Dave tried to convince Jan to join him once he had got used to being back on the boat by himself. 'We have to move on, darling,' he'd say, and try to lure her with the promise of fresh, ocean air and fish burgers from the marina fish shop.

'I think he would've liked my company and support at that sad time,' Jan admits. The couple got into tense conversations about it, in which Dave would tell her that they couldn't abandon the boat, that they'd worked so hard for this sort of lifestyle and that they had to allow themselves to try to have fun again.

When the Griffiths eventually did get out on *Honey May*, the experience was almost more fretful than it was worth. Losing Sophie overboard in an instant had driven it home to Dave how easy it was for accidents to happen out there. He'd always been cautious and even a little nervous on the boat, but now he wondered if it was possible to be careful enough. He would talk to Bridget about how he kept imagining what it would have been like if they'd lost a person overboard. 'It scared the crap out of him,' says Bridget.

Dave became anxious about making sure that everyone was where he could see them while the boat was moving. He spent a lot of his time looking over the edge of the flybridge and reminding everyone on board not to move around too much while the boat was in motion and not to stand close to the edge. He refused to have any more than five people on board. 'If he couldn't see someone, he would freak out,' says Bridget. 'It turned out to be not such a fun thing for him any more.'

But Dave was determined to get back out there. He knew that trying to regain his confidence on the boat was the only way to get through his grief. He told himself and Jan that they still had each other, and they continued their routines, working, cooking, planning overseas trips, breakfasting at Oscar's every day. But a major part of their lives was missing, and they both knew it.

9

Sophie Takes
Another Swim

At some point after Brian Kinderman's encounter with her and two or more months since she'd been flung into the wild, Sophie Tucker readied for another swim. It had been months since she'd fed on a steak and months since she'd had her red bowl of water waiting for her whenever she was the least bit thirsty. As far as Keswick residents knew, she was getting scrawnier and mangier by the day. She might have been digging holes and sucking up any water left in the forests, but the island was still experiencing a dry spell, so it couldn't possibly have been much. It didn't seem likely that she'd been sneaking up to the houses for a drink from potted plants, especially since no one had seen her. Brian's pursuit of the dog was the only substantial interaction anyone had had over there but no one on Keswick doubted that the mysterious hound was having serious trouble finding sustenance – there just wasn't enough food on the island for a grown dog to survive without coming into the houses. It was already scrawny when Brian saw it; it must have been getting worse.

When she was sniffing through the hills and the bush day in and day out, she must have been hanging on for a whiff of meat and gutted when this smell consistently eluded her. That was the smell that would have meant some much needed fat on her bones. But eventually she must have learnt to navigate a new set of scents. She was a cattle dog after all, bred to hunt and control animals far larger than herself. Whether it took a week or a month, at some point, Sophie's hunger had to have got the better of her and turned her into a huntress.

The problem was that on Keswick there wasn't a lot for a dog to hunt.

She was probably finding bird eggs or catching pheasants, scrub fowls or curlews, all of which Sophie knew from the backyard at home. Her paw prints on Arthur Bay suggest she was spending part of her days ferreting around the rocks of Keswick's beaches, catching the scuttling crabs with her tongue and trapping scurrying skinks with her paws as they attempted to disappear between rocks.

Perhaps she managed to catch a monitor lizard, creeping up on it in the sun and using her paws to pin it down by the tail or claw before biting its head off. She'd have had a good meal that way, but it would have been risky. Monitor lizards are fast, stealthy and can be vicious if they feel they are in danger. A swipe or a bite at Sophie could have injured her terribly.

She might well have gone fishing. She loved to swim and must have been feeling increasingly confident in the water; she probably took dips for reasons of both hygiene and refreshment. There are hundreds of fish on the fringes of Keswick, some of them gorgeous to look at, but many of them would have been too small to provide a whole lot of sustenance for a carnivorous dog. At high tide, though, meaty fish, like the sweet lip emperor and blue tusk, hover near Keswick feeding themselves on the shoals of tiny fish. Sophie hadn't fished before but the stealth lessons she'd had from Jordy in how to claw down birds might have kicked in. Perhaps Sophie learned to pin a slower, bigger fish down with her paws or to take a bite at it beneath the surface of the water. She might have got lucky and occasionally found some part of a fish washed up on the beach.

What is known is that Sophie was not looking good when Brian saw her less than two months after she went missing from *Honey May*. She was skinny to the point that her ribs were visible, a little dusty, and her face was drawn. She wasn't aggressive or threatening in any way. She was edgy but inquisitive, suspicious and coy. She wasn't healthy looking but also not that bad. Had Brian had a chance, he'd have plied her with food, but seemingly that wasn't on Sophie's agenda.

Sometime around 13 December, Sophie may have finally awoken to something similar to the smell of meat. The smell, which Jero swears he can sometimes pick up while paddling near St Bees, was most likely that of goats. It's thought that goats were introduced to St Bees and other islands up Australia's east coast in the nineteenth century, by sailors, as a food source for others who ran into trouble and needed to moor on one of the islands until help was on its way. As goats are wont to do, they have bred and continue to breed. So, in 2007, the QPWS Mackay office decided that the goats posed too great a threat to the native flora and fauna, and that the best form of action would be to gradually eradicate them.

'When we first started we were probably getting six hundred in one cull,' says ranger Ross Courtenay. In three years, the rangers rid St Bees of over two and a half thousand goats, mostly using helicopters to shoot from the air, but also with some land control. The eradication programme model was similar to that adopted in the Galapagos Islands, where eighty thousand goats that were threatening the environment for the island's native tortoises, were eradicated in just fifty-two months. To complete their task, the rangers used Judas goats – animals that had been captured and fitted with radio collars that inevitably found their kind and led the rangers to the herd. For the more wary male goats on St

Bees, QPWS marine park rangers use sterilised females to lure out the tougher guys.

Animal activists might cringe, but the Parks and Wildlife Service had to choose between feral goats and native flora and fauna – the goats have wreaked havoc on the island's vegetation, which has had all sorts of spin-off effects, such as mini-landslips, which threaten to spill soil into the ocean, affecting the water quality of a wider part of the Great Barrier Reef. The goats, hungry grazers that they are, have also all but devoured the seedlings of the blue gum and poplar gum trees, which the St Bees koalas eat.

If she wasn't smelling goats on Keswick Island, it's also possible that Sophie was smelling water coming from across the Passage. Unlike dry Keswick, St Bees has a number of natural springs. Locals know the story of the Bussuttin family who owned Keswick and St Bees in the early part of the twentieth century and initially used them both as farmland. They had horses and sheep and cattle on both islands but the animals on Keswick would frequently swim the Egremont Passage at nightfall to get to St Bees, where the family lived. It became clear to the Bussuttins that the animals could sense the water over there.

So Sophie, possibly lured by the smell of either goats or water, prepped herself for another swim. Her survival instincts must have been screaming at her that time was running out; she had to get to the smell of sustenance and she must have known that her only way there was back across the channel, the Egremont Passage that she had likely already braved at least once before.

The Egremont Passage is four hundred and eighty metres at its narrowest and just over a kilometre at its widest. Luckily for Sophie, she could never have known that it has claimed several grown men's lives. In January 2007, two years previously and at the same time of year that Sophie swam it, herself, a search went on in the Egremont Passage not an hour after sixty-five-year-old skipper Roy McKibbon dived in to fix an anchor rope attached to his fourteen-metre yacht, *Finesse,* and failed to resurface. Locals got into tinnies to search the Passage, with no success, until the Search and Rescue folk requested that everyone clear the water, realising the possibility of more danger. For three days, Volunteer Marine Rescue workers, along with an Australian Customs vessel full of police divers, searched in 25-square kilometre grids. A 50-kilometre aerial search was also conducted. Waves were at three metres high and the current was rushing at ten knots. McKibbon, who had sailed around the world in *Finesse,* was never found.

Most recently, in September 2010, locals awoke to the sound of helicopters and small planes circling overhead and boats motoring in the Passage. A twenty-one-year-old Irish tourist had disappeared the evening before from the fishing trawler, *Guiding Star,* that he'd been hired to work on just four days earlier. The man went off to the upper deck level to take photos and never came back.

The crew sounded the alarms. Helicopters, police boats, small aircraft, State Emergency Service workers and Volunteer Marine Rescue workers from Mackay and Airlie Beach searched for seven days to find him. By the fourth day, they were looking for a body; any remnants of the boy that his family could say goodbye to. To no avail. He was last seen at five p.m., camera in hand and the glint in his eye of a tourist who believed he was in paradise.

The residents of Keswick Island wouldn't dream of swimming in Egremont Passage and only the keen ones would dare to even paddle it in a kayak at anything other than the hour between low and high tide, when the water is perfectly still.

'I wouldn't like to swim it,' says Brian, who snorkels in the Passage at the cusp of the tide. 'All of a sudden I can start to feel the current,' he says, of the moment when the tide picks up and it's time for him to get back to shore. 'You really need the flippers just to get out of that current. Once it's going it makes it very difficult.'

Jero Andrews, who propels a blokart – a buggy powered by a windsurfer sail – up and down Basil Bay beach just for fun, and races against his Mackay mates (often, he admits, coming a distant last),shakes his head at the prospect of swimming it, himself, let alone Sophie. He monitors the tides on a daily basis and, like Brian, will only get his wave ski out on the Passage in the first or last hour of a tide, when the water is slowing to a still. 'Some days I worry that I won't be able to paddle the three hundred metres back to shore, the tide is so strong,' he says. Currents through Egremont run to the south towards Mackay when the tide is coming in, and north when it's outgoing, up towards the vast Coral Sea.

The tides aren't the only problem. Keswick residents have seen hammerheads, bronze whales and tiger sharks swimming in the Passage, some of them taking residence there for months at a time and scaring off the protected and fragile green sea turtles who lose flippers and their lives.

All these stories feed the Griffiths' horror when they have to confront how close and how often Sophie came to danger after she disappeared off *Honey May*. Sophie wasn't afraid of the water, though any sane human would have been after the ordeal she had suffered at the behest of the ocean. She was still a sea dog and a very experienced one by that point. If the paw prints on the beaches that various Keswick residents spotted are anything to go by, she was swimming most days. The Griffiths imagine her trotting into the waves and swimming around in circles with her tongue lapping out and her ears alert. It would still have been a therapeutic feeling, the salt and cold crunch of the water cleaning her fur and skin before she ambled back onto shore and shook it all out.

So on the December day that she took the channel from Keswick to St Bees, Sophie wouldn't have had to weigh it up too much – how far it was from Keswick to the smells on St Bees, how fast the current in Egremont Passage was really rushing. Had she been able to comprehend that the tides around Keswick in December and January are the highest that they are all year, she might have lost her nerve. Had she realised that she'd be swimming against currents of five to eight and possibly ten knots, which is about eight to fourteen kilometres an hour – sometimes faster through the channel – she might have stayed on Keswick. But she was a dog and her nose was leading her.

Whether or not she had been tracking the tides in preparation for her swim is impossible to know. It's not out of the question, though: local rangers tell stories of seeing wallabies on the popular resort Hamilton Island, sixty kilometres northwest of St Bees, gaze out to sea for days before leaping into the water and swimming a kilometre to neighbouring Dent Island.

What is certain is that, for Sophie, the dangerous swim was a matter of life or starvation. It's highly possible that, having covered up to ten nautical miles of ocean in deep shock after falling overboard, and having spent over fifty days with time to spare to watch the tides come in and out of the Egremont Passage, Sophie had worked out when the water was at its friendliest. She might have sat on the shore for hours, watching the sea rise and fall. Whether it was luck or planning, anyone who knows anything about Sophie's ordeal believes that she must have swum the Passage at low tide, because the water was just too fierce at high tide – its frequent casualties proved it – and would either have swept her out to sea or crashed her up against the coral near the islands.

'She had to have done it when the tides were slack,' says the Griffiths' seaman friend Warren Hill. 'She was pretty clever, she wouldn't have done it at high tide.'

'I'm just fascinated by the fact that the dog made it across,' says Sophie's vet, Dr Rowan Pert, who has also been an avid diver throughout the decades he's lived in Mackay, and who knows the odds against Sophie were astronomically high.

'It's amazing with all the currents out there,' says ranger Ross Courtenay, who has spent a lot of his working time out on Keswick and St Bees. 'To swim against the current and make headway is an achievement for anyone. The chances of a dog swimming even a kilometre or two from one island to the next, well, the chances of success are not good.'

Ross's colleague, Steve Burke, is in complete agreement. 'Mate, it was a great effort, really,' he says. 'Luckily, her breed, they're good swimmers, which would have helped her a lot. But to swim Egremont Passage . . .' Steve's look is full of awe, 'she must have been smelling goats. It would have been a matter of life or death, otherwise there's just no way she could have made it.'

Sophie would have swum for at least an hour, plunging into a vigorous stroke the minute she cleared Keswick's coral. She'd have stretched her head clear out of the water, moving her short legs in strong strokes, breathing heavily through her nose. She would have needed to keep her breath calm and her mouth shut. It would have been so easy to panic as the currents swirled and tugged at her body. But, extraordinarily, Sophie survived the potential predators and the strength of the ocean once again. As she clambered onto shore, she may have sustained cuts from rocks covered in oyster shells and coral that can slice flesh as if it were butter, although seemingly nothing too deep or severe that she couldn't lick and wash it into healing.

Either way, some time close to two months after washing up equally ragged and pumped with adrenaline on Keswick, Sophie found herself on the beach of yet another gorgeous, tropical island – alone, but this time in slightly more familiar territory. She had been near this island before on *Honey May*.

Once on land, she probably wasted no time searching for the smells that had enticed her – the goats or the water. There may still have been goat carcasses from the eradication programmes, left to decompose into the soil system. Goat farmers and processing plants in the area had been invited to come and pick them up for free as part of the programme, but had declined, as the travel out there made the enterprise less than cost effective. So after every cull, whole carcasses weeping blood from a shot wound lay close to St Bees' shores and in different locations up through the mountains, where the Judas goats had led the rangers and their rifles. Sophie wouldn't have been the first to find them; the eagles and the monitor lizards were all attracted to the carcasses, an abundance of easy food.

Feeding on a dead carcass was not something Sophie had done before. Apart from her months on Keswick, where the largest creature she might have slayed was an unwitting lizard or bush hen, she had never had to deal with the mess of intestines, the sorting through good and bad bits of a fresh kill, and she had not had to stalk a live creature and end its life to survive. In her bravado at home, sneaking up on birds or lizards was all a bit of fun. Her stomach wasn't empty then. Sophie had never brought home a decapitated gecko or a possum between her teeth, though she had definitely destroyed many a clueless peewee.

The Griffiths wonder whether she'd have approached a carcass with the same caution that she did the fish they pulled up onto the deck of *Honey May*. She would sniff her way cautiously up to the seemingly lifeless thing, then jump back if it flapped, looking around at her family as if to say, *Did you see that?* It was quite a leap for the Griffiths to imagine their girl going from that curious reticence, the sort of gentle enthusiasm for the wild world that is the luxury of domesticated dogs, to a calculated hunter, whether of living or freshly dead flesh. Their gentle house pet who loved nothing better than to rest her chin on Bridget's lap for hours, ripping into the bloody carcass of a baby goat? Let alone pinning it down for the kill?

The idea makes both Jan and Bridget uncomfortable, especially Bridget, who would like to think that Sophie would have killed only out of desperation. But the fact that she may have hunted for the sake of her own survival is also a matter of pride and admiration. She had dingo in her, after all, a side of the cattle dog ancestry (much argued about) that has been known to betray a working dog's otherwise disciplined ways by compelling some to rip into the animals they are charged with herding. Dingoes are natural hunters with extreme savvy and an unrelenting drive towards survival. It is just one of the breeding influences that has imbued Sophie's breed with essential aggression and tenacity. The latter trait, at least, Sophie exhibited over and over again during her time in the wild.

By the time she reached St Bees and its doomed goats, she would not have had a good meal for nearly two months. Whether she could possibly have slayed a goat herself or simply fed from a carcass, that first feed, the flesh and the guts and the blood must have been heavenly. After having to chase creatures on Keswick with very little meat on them and possibly going for days without finding anything, Sophie would have managed to make her way to a meal with some significant protein. Her belly would have been acidic and in much torment by the time she made it to St Bees, and whether it was the backbone of a decaying goat or the whole of an unsuspecting kid, those feral animals would have been the only solution out there for a carnivorous pup who refused to go to humans. That, and the fresh water running down from the mountains in St Bees' streams.

She might have risked her life to do it, but castaway Sophie had followed her nose to red meat and something to wash it down with.

IO

Puppies Make Everything Better –
Ruby Arrives

As the weeks since Sophie left their lives turned into months, Jan and Dave were still not coping well in Mackay. Jan was spending more time at the office than she had when Sophie was waiting at home for her, finding every excuse to stay and check on another invoice or gossip with Dave's then assistant, Megan. But all the sparkle had gone out of life. Luke, who came over for dinner at least once a week, had to watch his parents drag themselves around, pretending that everything was fine. 'They were moping about,' says Luke.

'I felt as though there was nothing really to look forward to,' says Jan, who wrestled with both her sorrow and the guilt over feeling so bad. There were so many worse things in the world to have to deal with. She had a wonderful family, she and Dave were still in love after all those years. But the hole was there. When she was at home alone in the afternoons, she turned the TV on for company as she went about doing chores or sat reading. She would try to go for walks on her own, putting her sneakers on and heading off down the road, but it felt forced and sapped her energy. Walking with no onlookers smiling her way in affectionate acknowledgement of Sophie made Jan feel as if she were living by rote.

The Griffith siblings were all concerned and Luke had an idea for how to cheer them up: another dog. It was simple. His parents needed a new dog to spoil and to rouse them from their misery. They needed a new pet to adore them and to adore back. They needed someone to talk to when the other was not around, an energetic soul to beg them for a run and to make them laugh again at their antics. And it had to be another cattle dog – the Griffiths would accept no other breed after all their beloved blue heelers. But perhaps a blue dog was a bit much – they might too easily be reminded of their pain and the loss. It would have to be a red cattle dog.

Not everyone was convinced a new dog, of whatever colour, was a good idea.

Bridget was especially against it. 'I just knew it was going to be so obvious that we were trying to distract them, especially getting them a red dog instead of a blue,' she says. Bridget was trying to get on with life in Brisbane, her student life was now in full swing and her social life finally flourishing as it had done in Mackay. She was also still in some denial about Sophie's disappearance. She had never got her head around how it happened and it was still too easy to imagine that it was all a dream. 'Part of me knew that getting a new dog would mean admitting that it was time to move on from Sophie.'

Luke decided to tell Dave about his idea. He'd been planning to surprise his parents with a new pup, but Bridget's reaction made him think twice.

Dave had similar feelings to Bridget. 'At first, Dad was completely against the idea,' Luke remembers. Gruff, practical Dave could not yet imagine loving another dog. 'No way!' he told Luke.

'A few days later, Dad calls me up and says, "Have you found one yet?" '

Dave looks a bit sheepish when reminded of this. 'No dog could ever replace Sophie but, well, it just wasn't any fun without a dog around,' he admits.

So, reassured and banking on the fact that the new pup would be a lovely surprise for Jan, Luke threw himself into the mission of finding a new cattle dog for his parents. He saw a litter advertised in the Mackay *Pocket Trader* and he and Heather drove to the farm for a look. The litter of blue and red cattle dog pups contained a female red who was both cheeky and lovely. Heather thought she would be perfect for the Griffiths.

The children of the breeders told Luke that the girl dog was their favourite and they'd nicknamed her Star for her flamboyance. 'Don't worry,' he told them, 'she'll be lounging in air-conditioned luxury in no time.'

Luke and Heather got Ruby ready for presentation to Jan, fitting her out in a shiny new red collar. But Jan already knew what was going on. 'It was obvious a new dog was on the agenda for Christmas,' she says now. But at the time she feigned ignorance. 'I didn't have the heart to say "we are not ready for this",' says Jan.

Luke and Heather sat Jan down at the poolside table one afternoon just before Christmas, put a towel over her head and dropped a wriggling Ruby, a ribbon wrapped around her neck, on her lap. Jan shrieked. Ruby ripped the towel from Jan's head with her teeth and licked her new owner on the face. 'Oh my God, oh my God,' Jan yelled, unable to contain her instinctive delight in this charming new puppy. Dave was rolling his eyes and smiling as Luke clapped him on the back, wearing a grin that said, *told you so!*

The initial euphoria of Ruby's arrival didn't last. Jan didn't admit for a long time that having a new dog around made her feel exhausted and sadder still. 'We would never have got Ruby ourselves because we had no inkling of desire to get another dog,' says Jan. 'We had only just gotten to the stage where, when we saw other dogs, especially cattle dogs, we either talked to their owners about what great dogs they were or commented to each other that they walked like Soph or they did something that Jordy would have done. But there was this feeling that no one would have healed the ache in our hearts.'

Sophie hadn't left Jan's mind for a second. She missed her and felt loyal to her and she couldn't fathom finding it in herself to become attached to another dog in the way she'd been attached to Sophie. And Jan knew that a new dog required energy – physical energy, but more importantly, emotional. It meant a responsibility to adore and delight in all the mischief as well as the devotion. For Jan, Sophie was still her number one pet. It was just too soon to extend her allegiance to another dog.

As if to confirm Jan's misgivings, Ruby was a typical cattle dog pup to boot, not the mellow creature Sophie had been but a tail-whipping cyclone that required a lot of attention. Unlike Sophie, Ruby was wholeheartedly enthusiastic and unquestionably needy. 'Ruby ran around like a wild thing. She was a lunatic, shredding, wrecking, jumping, tearing through the gardens and eating the plants,' says Jan. 'Not like Sophie at all and oh, it was hard to take.'

In mid-December of 2008, shortly after Brian saw the mysterious blue dog near the airstrip, Jan and Dave were starting to realise that their new daily mission was going to be getting used to the newest addition to their family. Just days into her life as a Griffith, the puppy was always ready for a wrestle, a pat, a lamb chop. 'Even if you take the batteries out, she's still going,' says Dave. The excitable pup was spending her time tearing around the yard, chewing on the shrubs in the garden, chasing birds and possums. And while she was bringing some much needed distraction to the grieving couple, she was also causing chaos. Jan and Dave were constantly bleeding from Ruby's sharp teeth accidentally scratching and biting them. Jan was covered in bruises from Ruby's claws digging into her when she jumped on her in the car, coming down the front steps, or while hanging out the washing. 'She didn't do anything mildly. She could hurt you without meaning to, she was just that desperate for attention,' Jan says. Jan and Dave were always on the look-out to make sure that Ruby wasn't destroying something. They'd find her dragging a palm frond the size of a dinner table round and around the garden.

Ruby spent her nights watching Jan and Dave's every move from outside the screen door. Their beloved Sophie had earned their trust and admiration and been invited into the house, onto the armchair and into the bedroom every morning, but Ruby had come nowhere near that privilege yet. She was too prone to jumping on people and objects with zero warning, piercing them with her sharp nails and ruining otherwise sweet moments by licking and pouncing with all her unbounded love and enthusiasm.

'It was like she was on Ecstasy,' says Bridget, who had a hard time bonding with Ruby. 'I was excited that there was a puppy but then I got home and thought, *You're a bit much.* Don't get me wrong, I thought Ruby was absolutely gorgeous, so cute. I just wanted her to stop – just calm down.'

It was hard for all the Griffiths, but especially Bridget, not to compare the rambunctious Ruby with the quieter, gentler Sophie. More placid and more stubborn, warm, intuitive Sophie was as happy with her chin on someone's lap as she was being thrown the tennis ball over and over for hours upon hours. Ruby, on the other hand, didn't sit still long enough for Bridget to pick her up and snuggle with her the way she'd loved to do with Sophie. She had an attention span not much longer than a goldfish's, so the game of throwing a stick or a tennis ball would last all of two throws. 'I wanted to say, 'that palm frond that you're eyeing off is still going to be there in ten minutes, can you just chill out so I can pat you?' Bridget says. But two pats on the head and Ruby would be gone, ready for, *what now?*

Bridget's first meeting with Ruby was when she came home for the Christmas holidays. She had a few days on her own to sound out Ruby before the rest of the family descended. Over the Griffith family Christmas, while everyone might have been comparing Ruby to Sophie and thinking about Sophie, no one was talking about her anymore. The kids hoped that one day it would be possible to revisit old memories, tell old stories, but they knew that they weren't there yet. There were still no photos of Sophie around the place and her name was understood to be all but unmentionable.

So the 2008 Griffith family Christmas marked the beginning of a new era with this tireless young red dog at their feet, crooning and drooling by their side as they dined, and jumping on the table or all over a Griffith, the minute someone turned their back. With everyone home for the holiday, Ruby was in her element. As the family kicked the three-day holiday off in the traditional way, with champagne for the girls, beer for the boys and games around the pool, Ruby was bouncing and slobbering and scratching wherever there was the slightest bit of action for her to be involved in.

Jan served up a tropical-tinged feast of fresh seafood salad with a homemade mango dressing followed by roast pork, roast turkey with 'Nan's special stuffing' as well as ham. There were veggies of roast potato, pumpkin, steamed greens, and to spice it altogether, cranberry sauce, apple sauce and gravy. Ruby got her fair share of the feast and then some, making herself more than available as the family celebrated for days, dining on leftovers, napping, and watching Australia's traditional Boxing Day cricket match.

Ruby was there for all of it, a pouncy, panting, tail-whipping force-of-nature dog, unfazed by reprimand and full of hope for fun times, all the time.

'If I had known then what I know now, I would have called her Ginger Rogers,' Jan recently said, adoringly. Instead, this is just one of the new dog's nicknames along with Fergie (after Sarah Ferguson, Duchess of

York), Red, Ruby Doobee, Rubes, Doobs, and Ruby Doobee Doo.

'I think I may initially have had some trepidation about getting them a new puppy,' admits Ellen. 'But in the end, I had to agree with Luke. Puppies make everything better.'

II

St Bees Island – Robinson Blue Dog

Peter Berck (who sadly died at the end of 2010) lived alone on St Bees for thirty years and had known stray dogs to come and go, left there by boaters who had to catch the high tide back to the mainland and return when it was safe to rescue their wandering pets. He'd also had dogs himself. Domestic animals were not technically permitted on the island but Peter's dogs had been such devoted allies that he justified it to himself. So when he got a call from Brian Kinderman on 16 December, telling him to look out for the blue dog that had been on Keswick and was now on St Bees, he was as excited as he was curious.

'That dog I told you about, the one I chased the other

week down Goat Road, it's over there with you now,'
Brian said to Peter on the phone.

The two men kept in regular touch to swap island
and Mackay gossip and have a friendly yarn. In early
December, Brian did have news: he had just a few days
earlier chased a blue dog from the airstrip to Basil Bay
and he didn't quite know how to feel about it.

'I don't know where it came from but Mike saw it a
few days before I did,' Brian had told Peter. 'I got the
rope out and swung it around but it wasn't having any
of it. I was too slow. Pathetic, mate.'

Peter chuckled. 'Those buggies will get you nowhere.'

Two weeks later, Brian called again, wanting to let
Peter know that a few of the visitors to the guesthouse
had reported seeing a dog skulking around on one of
the beaches on St Bees, across the channel, when they
were standing on the deck drinking their morning
coffee. The guests had marvelled at the sight of a lone
dog on the isolated beach over there. Who did it belong
to? It looked like it was catching crabs on the rocks.

Brian had filled his guests in on the whole story, how
the Keswick locals had been seeing the dog on their
island and wondering who it belonged to. No one had
been able to catch it. The dog was obviously tough and
was being elusive, but did not seem to be dangerous. It
was clearly someone's pet and most likely abandoned.

Brian had been amazed to hear from his guests that
the dog was on St Bees now. It must have swum right
across the Passage. It seemed unbelievable that a dog

could manage that feat – no one was silly enough to try to swim Egremont. This animal was starting to seem like some sort of super-dog. Every time someone encountered it, it was getting up to something unbelievable. Keswick people had been thinking that it was only a matter of time before they saw the dog in or near one of their houses. Now it was on St Bees? All this made for some exciting dinner table conversation for Brian and Lyn's guests. Wasn't the Passage dangerous? Weren't there sharks? How did a dog get across?

'It must be smelling food,' Peter told Brian. 'And remember, there's water over here. You guys have nothing over there.'

'Yep, it's true,' Brian conceded, laughing, knowing Peter was having a bit of a dig. *My island's better than your island.* 'It's looking pretty scrawny but it's a tough old thing. I don't know what it's living off but it didn't seem to want to befriend us. Maybe you'll have more luck.'

There was no doubt that a dog had a better chance of survival on St Bees than Keswick. The incredible thing was that this dog seemed not only to have worked that out, but to have done something about it.

St Bees Island looks from above like the fertile, primitive setting for a dream getaway that could go horribly wrong, a mostly deserted tropical island with scattered mangroves, palm trees, and a majestic shoreline from which visitors look out over to Keswick Island and the

Coral Sea beyond. Its steep hills are layered with rock and vegetation and only sensibly tackled with hard yakka, ankle-supporting boots. The north Queensland wet season ensures that, from January to May, St Bees is thick with eucalyptus trees and lush-leafed rainforest vegetation but the ground is covered in several species of wiregrass, its long blades capable of lacerating even the toughest of bare legs. All around the island there are mini beachfronts – bays the shape of fingernails with rock-strewn sand and mangroves. The water is as warm and blue as a hotel swimming pool, but in many areas, whipping with currents. At low tide, the bays become scratchy, muddy inlets. Boulders edge these beaches and are covered in oysters good for eating if someone has the tools and the time to wade into the water and extract them. This needs to be done at low tide, though, or the gatherer runs the risk of being knocked about by the tides and into the island's fringing coral banks.

Homestead Bay is the island's only developed area, if one could call it development. It is a roughly one-kilo-metre strip of beach with three stucco, ramshackle houses built randomly of brick, tin or timber, a couple of them with wobbly verandas from which to look out on the sunsets over Keswick and the Coral Sea. Whether motoring in on a tinny or flying overhead, Homestead Bay looks like paradise, something like the abandoned tropical island where a teenage Brooke Shields stowed away with her hunky cousin in *The Blue Lagoon* in the eighties. Tall, unkempt palm trees – a few of them that have stood there for at least sixty years – line the bay. Old generators, sand buggies and the occasional temporarily abandoned plastic toy are cosy evidence of the life of the Berck family.

The Bercks are some of just a handful of leaseholders of Homestead Bay over the past century. Peter Berck, the eldest of five Berck siblings, was a lean, pale-skinned man in his late fifties who lost his legs as a teenager as a result of electrocution. He and two of his mates were carrying an aluminium flagpole across a golf course in the town of Ann Arbor, Michigan, where Peter grew up. The accident occurred just before his family was due to leave for their native Australia, where Peter's father, Lionel, had purchased an island in tropical Queensland – St Bees.

Lionel Berck was fascinated by the island's history (and eventually wrote a book about it). It had been owned since 1907 by the large and innovative Bussuttin family, who raised cattle and sheep there, built gorgeous colonial houses and brought koalas over from Proserpine, just south of Mackay – possibly as pets and possibly to save them from the then-popular sport of koala shooting. Lionel Berck bought the Homestead lease in 1968 and the family used it as a second home. In 1979, Peter decided that his needs and his temperament were more suited to life on the remote St Bees and he moved to the island permanently. In 2006, Peter's younger brother David and wife Carolyn took over the lease from Lionel, with a group of their friends.

Peter was a dog person, through and through, so when he hung up the call on 16 December from Brian on Keswick, he was, in fact, looking forward to seeing his new neighbour. Years before he became an island dweller, he and his four siblings had spent childhood and adolescent weekends and school holidays on St Bees, along with their dog, Whiskey, a blue cattle dog just like Sophie. Whiskey often used to try to follow the family across the dangerous Egremont Passage when the Berck boys motored over to Keswick to mow the island's 480-metre long airstrip for pocket money. They'd have to stop the motorboat, scoop up Whiskey from the water and turn round to take her back to Homestead Bay to shut her in the house, so she wouldn't follow them and risk serious injury in the Passage.

Aside from the few disciplinary setbacks, Whiskey was one lucky dog. When the Bercks weren't mowing the Keswick airstrip, they were over on St Bees playing beach cricket, learning to catch tiger sharks and ignoring the swarms of feeding mosquitoes as they fell asleep under the palm trees that lined Homestead Bay. All the while, Whiskey was there, barking at sea eagles, tormenting the thousands of shiny brown geckos that scuttle and sunbathe on the island's rocks, feeding on mosquito corpses and chasing the waves as the tides came in.

Peter had had other dogs out on the island since he'd made his life there – dogs that also followed him everywhere. After Whiskey, there was Knickers, a black female cattle dog cross who had a litter of pups on St

Bees in the 1980s. David Berck had to fly over to take the litter to Mackay after Knickers carried them all up into the Bees' mountains for supposed safety. Then there was another female blue cattle dog whose real name was Zeuch, but for some reason Peter and all his visitors nicknamed her George. Both Knickers and George were less interested in chasing koalas and wallabies than they were in sticking by their loving owner's side, and while they revelled in island life, they, like Sophie were loathe to be far from their owner.

It had been a while since he'd had dogs though and Peter spent most of his days alone on the island. He kept himself busy, spending most days around his shed, fixing things, talking on the phone, drinking a beer or a glass of port here and there, and more often than not, searching the Internet for music. Whatever he was doing, he had music coming out of his giant subwoofer speakers. The volunteers who came to check the koalas on the island always knew when Peter was in the mood for a party when, from the top of St Bees' hills hundreds of metres away, at around four p.m., they'd hear the sounds of Creedence Clearwater Revival or the Bloodhound Gang blasting from Peter's shed. Peter spent chunks of his solitary time on the island digging up hits that had disappeared and bands that had fallen into the shadows, and priding himself on knowing every tune that had ever hit the Top 40 charts. He had over 2000 CDs on display in the Bees shed, alphabetised and each with the original cover art.

It was 18 January when Peter Berck first saw Sophie standing on the marshy flats of Homestead Bay at low tide, not a hundred metres from his front door. While Peter knew his obligation was to report this mysterious blue dog to the rangers when he saw her, he was some-what reluctant. He knew that, if the dog had gone feral and was impossible to capture, it would have to be shot. That January day when Peter Berck first saw the wolfish dog, he had a feeling about it. He even named it: Robinson Blue Dog. This dog was tough and by all accounts had been surviving on its own for quite a while.

It was a blue heeler; he was pretty sure, the same breed as Whiskey and George, though with a woollier coat, and far less trusting. It was standing with its back to the ocean, looking through the palm trees up at Peter as he shuffled out of the large, open shed.

Brian had told him when they'd spoken weeks earlier that the dog had been looking more and more dire every time it was spotted over on Keswick. Peter could see that it still looked thin – the ribs were showing and it looked drawn around the chin and eyes, but it didn't look sick. Its fur was thick and full of colour. Peter was relieved to see that by the looks of things, it had found at least some food on St Bees.

But when Peter whistled to it, the dog did not come bounding over, tail whipping, tongue flapping, ears perked the way his dogs used to, sometimes knocking people back a few steps in their enthusiasm. Robinson Blue Dog looked at Peter, looked away, looked at Peter, then started running. It broke into a gallop, its hind legs meeting its front, heading off to the north part of the island, towards Shark Point and into the hills of St Bees.

Sophie had arrived in time to revel in the island's abundant population of blue tiger butterflies, elegant big-winged creatures with swathes of electric blue across their glossy black base. These butterflies flutter all over St Bees most of the year but, in January, seem to multiply and descend upon Homestead Bay, floating about the daytime skies like confetti, collecting in the palm and the melaleuca trees. They head for anything damp to rest on, such as Peter's washed clothes hanging on a makeshift clothesline, or maybe Sophie's fur after a swim. Did she notice them? The marvel of a butterfly is not lost on dogs – there are stories of working dogs losing their stubborn focus on a four-hundred kilo cow at the sight of a butterfly or a dragonfly winging by. Perhaps, as Sophie rolled on the beach in the mornings or under a tree when the sun became too hot in the afternoon, she'd be stopped or awoken by a butterfly landing on her. It's the sort of image the Griffiths would like to envision to temper all the thoughts of the fear and distress she must have experienced. Jan, herself, has had moments of delight watching these butterflies on the family's trips to Keswick and St Bees, admiring them looking dazzling in the sunlight, landing on leaves and each other, and making elegant silhouettes against the purpling cloudy skies in a brewing wet season.

Beyond the goats, the butterflies, the lizards and the wallabies that Sophie must have seen during her jaunts into the hills, she must also have known there was human life on the island. Even before she locked eyes with Peter that January morning, she would have smelt it and also heard it.

During the day, as Sophie roamed the island, she'd have heard Peter's music in the distance and perhaps felt calmed by his presence. When there were no choppers or small planes flying overhead – the local news chopper scouting for scenery shots, perhaps, or visitors dropping in to Keswick for a weekend – Sophie would have heard the beat of Peter's tunes pouring into the tropical sky, which might have been one way that she avoided mistakenly entering Peter's space when he was around. She would also have been hearing the sound of a four-wheeler Argo buggy, a battered blue thing that roared like a Harley Davidson. Peter had been hooning the mobile around the island for decades when he needed to venture beyond the main camp, roaring up the hills and across sand.

So on 18 January, she finally made herself known to the person she must have been able to hear and sense. Though she didn't ever appeal to Peter for friendship or rescue, Sophie seemed to have made her way towards him deliberately. It would seem that Sophie wasn't looking for a chat or rescue but that she did need the sense of company. She wanted to be close to people but at a safe distance. That Peter was friendly but not overly concerned about her presence was perfect for her to take comfort in from afar.

Sophie and Peter had something in common: both of them wanted to be left alone as long as there was human contact close by.

Over the next few weeks, Peter would see the Robinson Blue Dog at various times throughout his days and nights, seemingly uninterested in the three ragged houses on Homestead Bay that might have provided it with shelter. He noticed that the dog was looking skinnier and skinnier, but was still not nosing up to his place for a meal, despite his best efforts to tempt it with bowls of dog food.

During their daily conversations, Peter told his brother David whenever he had seen the dog and the brothers would talk about what it might be eating. There were still plenty of goats out there and what about the wallabies? It didn't seem to be getting into any of that, otherwise it would be looking plumper. This meant that the dog had to be someone's pet, abandoned or lost, or it would be running far wilder.

Despite its scruffy state, Peter noticed that the dog moved smoothly and swiftly, passing by the scattered mangroves on the shore of Homestead Bay at low tide. It always looked alert and purposeful. Its ears were perked but for a flop in the left, its paws moving lithely. In the evenings sometimes, he'd see it coming over the dark rocks on the north side of the island where Shark Point disappears around the corner directly across from

Keswick and where St Bees becomes a series of boulders and bays. It was usually morning the few times
Peter noticed the dog making its way from Honeymoon
or Stockyard Bay on the south side, back over to Shark
Point and then disappearing around the shoreline or up
past the edge of the forest. The dog seemed to be getting
around but Peter figured it was making its bed somewhere over near Honeymoon Bay or perhaps somewhere
behind the abandoned line boat on Stockyard Bay.

He could tell from paw prints and frequent sightings
of the dog's hindquarters as it scuttled away at the
sound of him, that it was gradually coming closer to the
house. He told David the latest, who, knowing full well
the danger posed by a dog to the island's delicate ecosystem, had decided to tell the QPWS marine park rangers
about the animal.

When the rangers first heard of the mysterious beast,
not long after Pete's initial sighting, their instinct was to
try to trap it. For that, they needed Pete to do some
groundwork. 'We said, "Pete can you try and befriend
it?" ' ranger Steve Fisher explains.

The rangers knew they'd be going over to St Bees in
late March and they were trying to work out how to
humanely deal with the dog. If Peter could tame it by
then, they could remove it from the island without too
much effort or grief.

But Peter's efforts weren't enough. The bowls of Pal
that he was leaving just off the path between the beach
and his shed were not being touched.

'It seems to be hanging around Honeymoon Bay,' Peter told Steve Fisher. 'But I can't get it to come in here.'

Peter would see the dog rolling around on the beach – Sophie was having at least a little bit of fun – and sniffing around the casuarina and palm trees, then nuzzling into rocks, probably fishing for food. But the dog eluded all his invitations to come closer. Several times, Peter whistled to the dog as he saw it run across the mudflats just after sunrise. But this only resulted in the dog bolting, or at least directly ignoring him.

Whenever one of Peter's mates visited him on the island, they too would whistle and yell, 'Hey boy!' if they saw the dog in the distance, but it usually broke into a run immediately. At some point in late February, Peter noticed a significant improvement in the dog's weight. Perhaps it had found a good feed, quite likely it was a goat or two.

Peter and the dog he'd named after the famous literary castaway enjoyed this stand-off for most of January and February. And Peter didn't push it. He was developing a healthy respect for this solitary creature and although he couldn't get it to interact, they shared an apparent awareness of each other. Peter felt an affinity with the animal who was choosing to go wild rather than make a friend. They were two solitary creatures on an island together.

In early March, Tropical Cyclone Hamish threatened to bear down on Mackay and the surrounding coast and islands. In the end, it wasn't nearly as bad in and around Mackay as the media first predicted. On its way towards the coast, it turned south and headed towards New Zealand instead of central Queensland. But it still reached category five and hit the area with wild rainfall and turbulent winds that snapped branches and loosened coconuts and hurled sand around, creating piles of debris all over beaches.

In Mackay, Jan and Dave huddled up in the room under the house, having closed all the windows and stowed the outdoor furniture. They sat inside and watched the rain lash down almost parallel to the ground, listening for cracks and thuds close to home. Ruby was in there with them, whimpering and fretting a bit at the frenzied energy and all the loud noises. Jan stroked her and assured her, 'It's going to be alright, Ruby Doobee.'

Over on Keswick, Brian and Lyn Kinderman had cleared the deck and propped boards up against the doors. Brian had joined a few of the others tying wire around the building materials on the construction sites. They were now feeling relatively safe, sitting inside with good supplies of Bundaberg rum. The guesthouse and Keswick's other residences were built to withstand up to category four cyclones, but even so, Brian and Lyn ended up losing the guttering and amassing some other minor damage, after days of 70- to 80-knot (150 kilometres per hour) winds, almost three times higher than the speed at which planes are prevented from landing on the airstrip.

On St Bees, Peter had followed his usual routine: go to bed and listen to music. He had never felt the need to make his way to the concrete cyclone bunker behind the south house nor to make a huge effort to tie chairs and buggies up. There are an average of four to five cyclones every year in tropical Queensland and the biggest danger out on the islands is branches flying like missiles through the air and roofs coming off houses.

Presumably, Sophie had also worked out a plan of defence, detecting at some point that the gathering winds were blowing palm trees at crazier and crazier angles and that the rain was obscuring the ordinarily crystal view of Keswick. She must have realised the weather was too wild for her to be outside and found shelter somewhere on the island, possibly around one of the houses. She could have sniffed around the decks of the south or north houses to make sure they weren't inhabited, then curled herself into a corner underneath, to be out of the rain and muffled from the roar of the wind. She might, alternatively, have dug a great big hole somewhere under a canopy of trees and nestled in for the duration of the storm under leaves and branches.

Sophie wasn't usually frightened of storms. She didn't exactly love thunder but neither did she fret and shiver the way some dogs do. Nonetheless, Jan and Dave had always had her in with them in wild weather. She would lie there next to them looking around, seemingly aware of what was happening, but the most anxiety they'd known her to show was barking occasionally when she heard a bang or crack in the distance. This was hardly preparation for being right out there in it, though.

Several days after the worst of Hamish hit St Bees, David Berck and one of the homestead's co-owners, Frank Debrincat, were out on the island cleaning up the coconuts and palm fronds scattered about the bay and making sure that the doors and roofing were still on the houses. David had flown over from Mackay to meet Frank. Peter had come through cyclone Hamish without incident, but he was suffering from throat cancer, and had very reluctantly left the island for treatment in Brisbane.

Frank headed down to the south house to check on its screen doors and big old table. The table was well protected under the deck roof and too heavy to be lifted by any but the most savage storm, but Frank just wanted to be sure. He made his way along the dirt and rocky path between the houses, winding around a corner and under overhanging trees. As he approached the old generator shed next to the path he was in his own world, thinking about the weather and the beauty of the island.

The shed, a green wood-panelled shelter with the windows and doors busted out, stands about two hundred metres along the path between Peter's and the south house, and still contains an old diesel generator that the Bercks used until they installed a newer, bigger one near the north house in the 1990s. The shed, rarely used, is warm and dark and full of spiders and crawly things and most likely a haven for snakes – none of them deadly. Most of the snakes on St Bees are non-venomous tree snakes, the sparkly green variety that spend their days slithering from one tree branch to the next and sleeping.

Just as Frank was passing the doorway, he got a fright. He heard a growling noise. He swallowed. There were white teeth baring from one of the dark corners of the shed and then he saw eyes and fur. The fur was thick and dark blue, ruffled up around the creature's neck as it growled at him, eyes ablaze, still lying down but its head raised from sleeping position, legs readying to stand if need be.

Shit, a wolf, Frank thought, panicking.

Frank had heard there was a dog on the island but he hadn't been thinking about it at the time and this beast seemed far more threatening than Peter had described. Frank wasn't about to give it more of a scare or a challenge. He was wearing his usual King Gee shorts, his legs bared, an easy target for an angry, scared hound to latch on to.

The beast continued to growl as Frank backed away, not taking his eyes off the animal's, which were still glowering from the corner of the shed. *It must have been sleeping there*, thought Frank. *What is it?* It was blue and furry and angry. It did look like a wolf. *But there aren't any wolves in Australia and even if there were, how had this one got to St Bees?*

As he moved away, the animal slunk out the shed door and bolted. 'That's the dog,' he realised, as he glimpsed its blue coat in the daylight and saw that it was more scared of him than the other way around. Frank took off in pursuit. He whistled and called out but the dog was long gone, somewhere over near Shark Point.

Frank went back to the main house to calm himself down with a cup of tea and to tell David Berck. 'I saw the dog,' he said. 'Scared me. I thought it was a wolf.'

'There *are* no wolves in this country,' David pointed out.

'It's furry and it's mean and it was in the generator shed. It was growling at me,' said Frank.

When David called Peter in the hospital and told him about Frank's scare, the issue of the dog escalated. When Peter and David got over a little giggle – *What was Frank thinking? A wolf?* – the brothers started to think that they were not going to be able to let this go for much longer.

'To start with, we just thought it was a dumped dog. Some yachties had come along and camped, couldn't find the dog that's run off, and left it there,' says David's wife Carolyn. But this was different. This blue heeler had been out there a long time, and it had scared Frank by growling and hissing.

Carolyn had already been concerned for the safety of her children, seven-year-old Hayley and five-year-old Tyler, who spent their time on St Bees running around barefoot and free, playing cricket on the beach or tearing up bush tracks to drink fresh water from springs, but her concern escalated after Frank's encounter.

David did a few quick searches around Homestead Bay and came upon the carcasses of several baby goats out in the bush behind the south house. These goat carcasses were a little closer to the main house than he felt comfortable with. They could have been left over from a past cull but they could also have been the handiwork of a very hungry, feral dog. 'If it was bringing down goats, then it was getting vicious. It had the taste for blood,' David explains. Between them, the Bercks realised that they needed to act soon to get the dog off the island. 'We didn't know whether the dog was a serious threat or not, but in any case, it was against the rules for it to be there, and we just couldn't take the risk.'

One way or another, Sophie's days as a castaway were numbered.

12

So Near and
Yet So Far

On New Year's Eve, 2008, over two months after
Sophie went overboard, Jan, Dave, Bridget and
Sammy, Bridget's roommate from Brisbane,
piled onto *Honey May* for a day out on the water. They
were headed for St Bees Island, to one of its little beaches
adjacent to Homestead Bay.

Jan and Bridget had suggested the trip when they
heard the weather report saying that the weather was
going to be divine even by Queensland standards.
Christmas was over with and this year the other Griffith
siblings hadn't stayed on for the rest of the holiday.
Usually they would all have been on their way to the
Eimeo pub for shandies and fish and chips, a New
Year's Eve tradition since Ellen and Matthew left home.

But this year, the others had arranged to go camping with mates, so going out on the boat seemed like the perfect way to spend a quiet New Year.

The day before the trip, Dave was dragging his feet. 'It wasn't like him at all,' says Bridget who, looking back, now realises that he was thinking about Sophie. Dave grumbled that he liked to plan for these trips further in advance. He muttered about how much work it was to get the boat ready and then to clean it afterwards. He reminded Jan that *Honey May* was having some issues – it was blowing out black smoke. It wasn't anything serious though, and Dave was usually so enthusiastic about his retirement hobby. Ordinarily it was Jan who rolled her eyes about all the work and all the money they funnelled into *Honey May*. 'Why can't the bloody thing just work,' she'd say sometimes. But it was New Year's and they'd had a hard couple of months and Jan thought they needed to get out of the house. She hoped that getting Dave out on the water would cheer him up and she was trying, after their talks about her lack of enthusiasm since Sophie's disappearance, to revive her own joy for the boat.

They compromised: rather than go all the way to their beloved Scawfell, they'd pop over to St Bees, which was at least half an hour closer. It wasn't Bridget's favourite destination – the beaches were rockier than on Scawfell and she'd never liked to swim in Egremont Passage. 'The water just whips through there,' says Bridget who on one family trip thought she'd try to swim across the channel to Keswick, just for the fun of it. 'I thought I could manage it but I ended up turning around. When the tide is moving, you have to swim at a diagonal just to keep yourself travelling straight. It was not fun at all.'

Jan told her to buck up, and reminded her that the beach was just as incredible as Scawfell's. At high tide, swimming in the bay just off the Passage was perfect. It got deep quickly and they could float around, looking up at the rock cliffs, and sometimes waterfalls, if it had been raining.

Besides, they were all working hard to get Dave excited, and so as long as he was prepared to go somewhere, Bridget was up for it. She wasn't going to be bratty.

But Dave was still not keen on the whole idea.

'He didn't even want to take the dinghy, which would have meant that we wouldn't have been able to go to the beach,' Bridget says. 'And I said, "no, we'll want to go to the beach. We'll make sandwiches, come on." He was kind of being a bit of a wet blanket about the whole thing, which was totally unlike him because he was always so proud to take us out.'

In the end, Bridget and Jan convinced Dave, partly just by being ready to go.

Jan packed the usual overabundance of snacks and drinks, chicken and some delicious baked treat that she had spent an afternoon putting together – Jan is famous for her chocolate slice and her caramel drops, buttery biscuits with a chewy dab of caramel in the centre. There was white wine and beer and plenty of Diet Coke for Jan to sip on when she was feeling seasick.

There was absolutely no question of taking Ruby. Unlike Sophie, she was simply too hyperactive to have on the boat. Not only would she drive them all bonkers with her rushing and scampering about, they would be terrified that she'd bounce overboard. But they knew now the speed with which something disastrous could happen and they weren't going to risk it again. As the family set off, leaving a very sulky Ruby behind, it was impossible not to think of Sophie, who had so loved being with them and so enjoyed the ocean.

The sky was glassed out with not a cloud and the ocean was completely calm. 'It was just beautiful,' says Bridget. It was another one of those flawless north Queensland days and it was hot, perfect for being splashed all over by *Honey May*'s wake of sea water.

They motored over to St Bees, which took them about an hour. Bridget and Sammy were taking photos of each other pulling silly faces on the front deck. Dave was quiet, driving the boat up on the flybridge and Jan was up there too, doing her best to quell the queasiness, munching on dried apricots and looking into the horizon. Jan couldn't stop getting flashes of *the trip* out of her mind. They were heading on virtually the same route and today was sunny and calm, as that day had started out. *One foot in front of the other*, Jan reminded herself. She was fighting not to allow still-tormenting memories to overtake the fun they could still have out there.

They moored the boat at the mouth of Egremont Passage and motored in to Vincent Bay, across the passage from Keswick Island, with all the picnic gear on the tender. Anyone sitting on Brian and Lyn's deck would have seen picnickers on the shore across the channel, just as they'd looked out and seen the dog sniffing about the shoreline weeks before. The beach, as most of the little inlets around St Bees are, was as much rocky as it was sandy. It was a lean curve of sand book-marked by rocky headlands and jutted with boulders covered in oyster shells. In low tide, the bay was muddy and scrappy and scattered with coral and oysters but at high tide, which they caught on this day, the water was incredible.

Bridget kept her mind off the comparison to Scawfell's white sand paradise by getting her video camera out. She had been taking comedy classes in Brisbane and had a budding career as a comedian, so she was making a mockumentary inspired by the iconic nature movies of David Attenborough, with Sammy as the star.

At some time in the afternoon, after the family had eaten lunch and while Bridget and Sammy were film-ing each other, over in a watery inlet separated from the main part of the beach by a sand dune, they heard a yell from Jan. She had gone on a shell-investigating mission around the beach. 'Come here, come here!'

she yelled. She was on the opposite end of the beach to the girls. At first, the family ignored her, figuring she was having an excited moment in her explorations. 'We thought she was just being her dramatic self and that she'd call out in a moment that it was nothing,' Bridget says.

Jan was fossicking about on the edges of the forest where it grew over the sand line at the back of the small beach. She was picking up shells, ducking in and around the scrub and each inlet of rocks and staying out of the sun – the overgrown ferns and windswept trees provided natural shade on the hot, hot day.

'Everyone, stop what you're doing, come quickly,' Bridget remembers Jan insisting. 'We thought she'd found a snake or a goat or something awesome like that.'

They sprinted over, Bridget calling out to Dave who was down by the shore checking over the tender that he'd pulled onto the beach. He, too, stopped what he was doing and ran over. Jan was standing amidst a clump of trees, wearing one of her huge sunhats and Hollywood-sized sunglasses. 'She was like, "I think I've found a goat's nest, isn't it eerie?" ' Bridget was embarrassed, in a charmed sort of way, that her mum was being so melodramatic. 'I was, like, *are you even my mum*? She was being all hippie and weird. There was nothing, just sticks and bones.'

Jan knew Bridget was teasing her but she insisted. 'Come here, *look* at this.'

Bridget glanced at Sammy, shrugged and moved

closer to the nest with her camera. In fact, it was a whole animal skeleton, head and all.

'I have this really peculiar feeling,' Jan said to Bridget. She had her hand on her heart and her face had paled.

Bridget looked at her mum and wondered what was going on. In the midst of her teenage embarrassment, Bridget didn't twig to what was going through Jan's mind. *Bones. Nest. Shelter. Sophie*, was whirling through Jan's thoughts. *Here were the remains of a goat and, if a dog had done it, could that dog have been Sophie?*

Jan was overcome with emotions she couldn't really explain. She had edged unwittingly up to the nest and stopped in her tracks. The carcass had a skull on it and it was about the size of a dog's head.

'I saw the shape of the head and, well I just stopped,' she explains now. *Oh my God, it's a dog*, Jan thought to herself, for a split second before she saw it was definitely a goat. Her heart started to ache. She clutched at it. It was as if all the grief of the past few months was facing her here on the beach at St Bees.

'I looked around and I looked up at the little rock gullies where there are waterfalls when it rains. Here was this goat that had died and I thought, *if Sophie made it here, she could have made herself a resting place, a nest.*'

Jan suddenly felt serene. 'If she'd made it here, she would have been protected,' she thought.

At the time, Bridget was no longer thinking about Sophie every time they went out on the water. Part of this was that it was still painful to think about her lovely puppy, stranded out in the water, hitting the wake of *Honey May*, suffering. But also, the fact of never really knowing what happened and never being able to say goodbye had prevented Bridget from facing the fact that she was gone. There was no tangible memory of her death to bring closure. Bridget's life in Brisbane was booming and, while she'd been back to Mackay several times and experienced home without Sophie, Bridget had dealt with the grief with a little bit of fantasy.

'Dad still had all her water dishes and so it was like, I don't know, she just wasn't there,' Bridget struggles to explain. 'It was as if she was on an extended holiday somewhere. I couldn't believe it. It just didn't seem like she'd actually gone.'

Jan, on the other hand, was dealing with the palpable absence of Sophie at home every day. Puppy Ruby was certainly offering up enough attention and diversion to lessen the loneliness of Sophie's absence. She had injected some much-needed frivolity into Jan and Dave's days. But she wasn't Sophie.

As the tide turned, ready to take them back to Mackay, the Griffith family packed the picnic gear and the blankets into the tender. Jan was still thinking about Sophie. 'It was an amazing feeling. It wasn't terrible but it really got me,' she says. 'I didn't tell anyone what I was really thinking because I knew it would just stir Dave up, and Bridget was in her own place.'

Jan stood on the shore and looked over to Keswick.

The tide was high, the water still sparkling in the heat of the afternoon. 'I just kept thinking, if she made it here, she might have survived.'

On board *Honey May*, as they came out of the Egremont Passage, Jan looked behind them over to Aspatria, a nautical mile away but very much visible from St Bees. She couldn't see Hesket Rock, although even remembering it was there brought the usual moment of anxiety. She didn't allow herself to really focus on everything that was swirling through her mind, but somewhere a thought flickered: *could Sophie have made it here?* She was a good swimmer and she was bullheaded enough to try it had she survived the fall overboard.

Jan didn't share her feelings with anyone. Dave and Jan were still barely mentioning Sophie's name to each other. They were at a point where they could have a warm sigh together at the sight of other blue cattle dogs that reminded them of Sophie. There were cattle dogs everywhere, passing by on the back of utes as Jan and Dave looked out of Oscar's windows in the morning, or snorting on the end of a lead as Dave took Ruby for walks. But Sophie's disappearance was still too tender to bring up casually. Jan knew that raising the idea with Dave of Sophie making it to St Bees would make him hurt, rather than hope. The chance of Sophie surviving a fall into the ocean so far from land was outlandish. It had been over two months since she'd gone overboard. How could she have survived all this time?

But nevertheless Jan left St Bees with an eerie feeling, one that never left her. Now, when she dreamt of Sophie, she saw her on beaches, running into the ocean off the shore.

What Jan and the others didn't know (or maybe Jan felt), was that Sophie was on St Bees that day. It was two weeks before New Year's Eve that Brian Kinderman's guests had looked out across the deck to see a dog rolling around on the very same beach that the Griffiths were picnicking on. Sophie could have been up on a knoll about a 200-metre climb from them, or she could have been fishing off the rocks on another one of St Bees' beaches. She was definitely there, though, and if she had looked out and seen *Honey May* or picked up their scent, she could have come scampering out of the bushes or around the rocks as the tide receded, wagging her tail, snorting and grunting, her tongue lolling in utter delight. 'I just imagine she would have run up to us, her hips swaying, thinking, *there you are, I've been waiting for you!*' says Jan.

The most likely scenario, though, is that Sophie was several beaches down, somewhere on the opposite side of Homestead Bay to where the Griffiths were, either resting under trees or lying in the water. It was a scorching day – Bridget was getting pink and red as she mucked about in her bikini – and Sophie, having recently pulled off another big swim to get to St Bees, must have been tired and hot. Most likely, she would

Views of the one kilometre beach and mudflats of Homestead Bay, St Bees, across which Sophie was spotted running throughout her months on the island.

Peter Berck's generator shed, where Frank mistook Sophie for a wolf.

The wrecked line boat at Stockyard Bay, St Bees, near the area where the park rangers trapped Sophie.

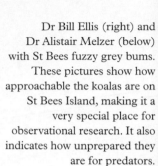

Dr Bill Ellis (right) and Dr Alistair Melzer (below) with St Bees fuzzy grey bums. These pictures show how approachable the koalas are on St Bees Island, making it a very special place for observational research. It also indicates how unprepared they are for predators.

Dr Alistair Meltzer (left) and volunteers radio-tracking koalas on St Bees.

Beach scrubs on Stockyard Bay, under which the rangers placed Sophie's trap.

Home at last! Just off the QPWS boat at Mackay Marina, Sophie takes off with Dave while Jan offers their hasty goodbyes and thanks.

Sophie's first day home! Lying in her favourite spot in front of the air conditioner.

Photo call 6th April 2009. Sophie makes headlines around the world.

Bridget, home on holiday, watches a spot of TV with Sophie.

Who's ready for a game?

Jan and Sophie play ball after dinner.

Sophie tires of ball games and retreats somewhere dark and a little quieter.

Jan, Sophie and Dave on their new boat, *Molly B*, at Mackay Marina.

Will you please throw the ball now, Dave?

Sophie and her new friend, Ruby.

Sophie and Ruby play games around the pool.

Sophie and Ruby, both allowed inside!

have been taking shelter somewhere. It's hard to imagine that, had she been anywhere close, she wouldn't have smelt her beloved family out. It's a stomach-churning thought for the Griffiths. The possibility of a reunion that day was far greater than any of them could ever have imagined.

13

St Bees Fuzzy Grey Bums and a Blue Dog

Sophie could never have known how close she had come to being rescued by the very people she had been waiting for all those weeks. When the Griffiths motored ashore to Vincent Bay, she'd been gone for over two months and still hadn't made any attempt to secure new owners. It would seem that Sophie, devoted Griffith family member that she was, was still holding out for Jan and Dave to come pick her up. So how did she miss them that day? St Bees was not a tiny outcrop of rock, by any means, but she'd been on that very same beach two weeks earlier and how far away could she really have travelled in her reportedly waning state?

Did she make her way to Vincent Bay again after the Griffiths left, and pick up on their scent? Did she sniff around the beach and detect Jan's sunscreen or Bridget's shampoo, indeed any of their familiar scents, and look up and about her excitedly? Did their scent inspire her with further motivation to keep going, keep surviving, knowing that they were out there, somewhere?

Then again, she'd only been on St Bees for two weeks the day Jan found the goat skeleton and had a sort of epiphany, and Sophie must still have been trying to adjust to yet another new environment. Perhaps she didn't go back to Vincent Bay at all or not until many weeks after the Griffiths had gone, by which time, their trail would have faded.

She'd spent nearly two months trying to survive on Keswick, only to consistently shed pounds as, day after day, she failed to find enough food and water to nourish her. That search would have been her overwhelming priority now. And it seemed that her movements were not entirely impulsive. Rather, Sophie appeared to be her calculating, cautious self out there on the islands. She had probably spent time preparing for the swim over to St Bees and once she arrived, she probably rested before setting off to explore the island, in search of her best chance at survival.

There were a lot of new experiences for Sophie on both Keswick and St Bees. The constant solitude and the hunt for food were the main ones. There were also so many smells to investigate – of tea trees and macaranga trees, of Keswick's bees and of St Bees' goats and their sun-soaked flesh. And on St Bees there were new noises too. Hours after night fell she would have woken to an entirely unfamiliar sound. She would have known the wailing, sorry moans coming from the curlews all over the island, from back home in Mackay. But overwhelming the cries of the curlews would be bestial sounds resembling a wild pig. They would start after midnight and last for hours, escalating from a guttural bellow to a loud, aggressive grunt. There would have been heavy breathing and almost gasping noises as the sound built into a crescendo.

Did Sophie set off along a bush track in search of this new, mysterious noise – another potential threat to her survival? Or did she huddle even further into her nest, be it in the generator shed or on a pile of eucalyptus leaves in some secluded spot? Sophie couldn't know it, but those eucalyptus leaves were the very substance sustaining the animal emitting the hearty noise. And what she also would not have known, at least at first, was that she was a far bigger threat to that creature than it was to her. That creature was a koala. And there were hundreds of them. The ones making the noises, the grunting and bellowing, the ones that were probably interrupting Sophie's sleep at night, were males.

Every year the St Bees koalas bring scientists and volunteers to the island, eager to study them. One of the regulars is zoologist Dr Bill Ellis, who has spent the better part of his past twenty years clambering up eucalyptus trees all over Australia, swabbing chunks from koala's ears and tongues or collecting fecal pellets to analyse back in Brisbane.

Bill (sometimes known as 'Bill the Koala Man') is a tall, laconic guy in his mid-forties. His scruffy salt-and-pepper hair is not unlike the colour of a koala's fur and his eyes are an intense blue, again, not unlike a koala's. Bill, along with his zoologist colleague Sean Fitzgibbon and ecologist Alistair Melzer, have been catching and studying the Bees koalas (otherwise known as teds, teddies and fuzzy grey bums) since 1998, when a fellow koala-lover and frequent research volunteer, Mary McCabe discovered one halfway up a tree while camping on St Bees.

'Until then, we didn't know there were koalas out here,' says Bill. Nobody had thought to look for koalas on St Bees, mostly because the island was so off the radar. Once Mary McCabe had paddled her sea kayak up to the Bees' Homestead Bay and told her friend, Alistair Melzer, that she'd seen one clinging to a tree during an afternoon exploration, they went on to discover that the St Bees koala population actually exists in a rare harmonious state, unafraid of human or animal threats.

Several times a year, the scientists island-hop off the coast of Mackay, from Stradbroke, Rabbit, Newry and the popular resort island, Brampton, then on to St Bees. They pack up metal poles and specimen jars, hiking gear and wide-brim hats and they put the word out to any locals who might be heading to a koala area and can give them a spot on their boat or plane. Over on St Bees, the scientists and their revolving army of volunteers, who come from all over Australia and the world, sleep in bunk beds in the south house's school-camp-like bedrooms. (Although if it's just Sean and Bill, they roll out their swags and sleep under the stars.) Everyone logs the day's info on laptops, stores their koala-luring poles and heavy boots, and winds down at night with steak and a few beers and endless games of dice, to the backdrop of curlew calls, bellowing koalas and rolling waves.

Koalas have been threatened for decades throughout Australia, mostly by land clearing. The Australian Koala Foundation estimates that there are 80,000 koalas left in the wild, possibly as few as 43,000, and there is research going on all over the country with the hopeful goal of creating a national solution that will save the species.

'We must be approaching the point where they are functionally extinct, where these creatures are not going to be able to continue at any sort of viable level,' says Bill, who sees Australia's ability to save these universally-loved animals as an end in itself, as well as a symbolic step towards preserving the planet. His optimism roller coasters as the years go by and he sees government plans come into action and disappear, and funds for koala research wax and wane. 'Try picking one element of the ecosystem that we'd really like to save – people want to save trees but it's not universal. With koalas, it's universal. Everyone looks at koalas and even if they know nothing about them, says, "oh, they're so cute we've gotta save them." We've got this species that lives quite close to us and which is quite resilient. Can we save it? It looks as though we can't.'

Bill tries not to dwell on the doom and gloom, and to stay positive. That's why the St Bees koalas are so important to his research. The koalas on the islands in the Cumberlands and Whitsundays are particularly healthy, and the discovery of the St Bees population has led to significant gains in knowledge. An estimated 300 koalas are living on St Bees, and almost as many have been tagged over the years by Bill and his colleagues. Koalas have come and gone in the St Bees community, munching on eucalyptus leaves and sleeping by day and, it would seem, making a racket by night. They are among the healthiest of Australia's diminishing population of koalas because they live outside of civilisation – without the smog of traffic, without the menace of wandering house pets, without the threat of development that replaces trees with buildings and koala-friendly paths with fences. The koalas on St Bees do have chlamydia, which, after their diminishing habitats, is the single largest threat to koalas' existence. But many of the St Bees koalas are asymptomatic and those infected don't seem to suffer as badly as their mainland compatriots. 'The bacteria doesn't seem to impact the population in the same way it does mainland groups,' says Bill.

Alistair, Sean and Bill track several things: the effects of illness, who has moved from this tree to that or from that part of the island to this, new babies and who has given birth to them – female koalas seem to start giving birth at the age of two and keep going, having one baby a year after that – and who is mating with whom. In the decade that Bill and Sean have been tracking St Bees' population, two of the female koalas have given birth to at least nine babies each and the scientists are fairly certain that all of them came from different fathers. 'That's a pretty cool piece of information,' says Bill. Nobody had speculated that this might have been the case, until Mary McCabe stumbled upon the St Bees teddies.

Sometimes the scientists spend their days climbing trees and rustling a plastic bag above the koalas. This trick drives them to the ground to be pinned down and swabbed, tagged, or otherwise inspected. Although occasionally, they attack the bag. Volunteers working with Bill over the years have lost parts of their fingers and sometimes even entire fingers. Bill, himself, has been nipped, but luckily the koala's incisors only got the fleshy part of his pointer finger – if it had been the koala's back teeth, Bill might be one finger short these days. He and Sean insist, though, that if a koala gets angry, it's because the catcher hasn't been careful enough.

The first person to get their hand on the koala gets naming rights, and the only stipulation is that the name begin with the next letter in the alphabet after the most recent koala noted in Bill's log book. Once the koalas have collars, the researchers are able to track them for years and years. As a result, Bill and the others frequently become attached to certain koalas.

Each time they arrive on St Bees, Bill and Sean try to prepare themselves for the possibility that one of their favourite koalas has died. Finding a dead koala is a professional hazard. 'It's a total bummer when you come across one of the real characters, the ones we've become attached to,' says Bill, who, when he turns up to Bees these days, is preparing himself to find Elizabeth, an eleven- or twelve-year-old koala, dead. 'But she keeps on keeping on,' he says, delighted. Bill and Sean mourned a female koala named Yellow a few years back, who appeared to have travelled several hundred metres from her usual tree to the spot where she died – something not often observed. Bill now tracks the movements and listens to the bellows of one of Yellow's sons, a fully-grown male named Stewy who was probably responsible for some of the bellowing that Sophie heard in the night.

Other times, the scientists spend their days lounging on the deck or visiting Brian and mates on Keswick and telling jokes. Then at night, they head into the hills, walking slowly over the crunchy bush paths to the spot where they know a koala is hanging about. They might crouch for hours beneath trees, trying to avoid being peed on (though Bill says that if you're going to get peed on by an animal, best it be a eucalyptus-eating koala). Their work at night is to try to work out what, exactly, is going on when these male koalas grunt and gasp and bellow into the darkness.

'We're sort of trying to work out who's talking to whom,' explains Bill. Are the males marking their territory: the deeper the bellow, the more virile the male? Koalas like to breed but they are also a solitary species and need to keep it that way or they'll claw and bite each other ferociously. Bill, Sean and their colleague Jason Wimmer, around the hills and knolls of St Bees, have recorded the koalas throughout the year, something they haven't been able to do in urban populations where noise from roads and backyards interferes with both the recordings and with the koalas' confidence.

In early 2009, over two months after Sophie had gone missing off *Honey May* and in which time, Brian Kinderman and Peter Berck had spotted her on Keswick and then St Bees, Alistair Meltzer made two trips to St Bees for research. He'd heard from the various sources – Brian, Peter, as well as Bill – that there seemed to be a dog on the island and they thought it was a cattle dog. The information put the scientist on alert.

'Having had a cattle dog of the same type, I know they can be efficient hunters once blooded,' says Alistair, who had gathered from his conversations with the Bercks that the dog might have been killing goats. 'I wasn't too concerned but I was curious. A dog on this island could be a threat to our study of the koala population,' says Alistair who, like Bill, also happens to have striking blue eyes and greying thick hair resembling that of a koala.

Alistair recalls noticing a change in the vibe of the

island's ordinarily unflappable swamp wallaby population when he was out on St Bees over the months that
Sophie was on the island. 'Over the previous decade the
swamp wallabies had usually been quiet and we could
approach to within a few metres of a mature animal,
although not a young one,' he recalls. 'But on those trips
at the beginning of 2009, all the wallabies would take
flight at first sight or sound of us.' In past years, Alistair
and Bill would have wallabies hanging about the south
house while the koala teams were in residence. They
were friendly, calm animals, who would hop up to the
kitchen's screen door or even up the three wooden steps
to the deck, completely unafraid of people. But Alistair
noticed that the wallabies were far more skittish during
the period that Sophie was on the island, more likely to
hop away at the sound or sight of him traipsing around
the hills and gullies with his camera.

If this was happening to the wallabies, what then of
the koalas?

The concern was that hungry Sophie might have
gone for a koala when her survival instincts had well
and truly set in. If she was hunting and killing goats,
there wasn't much to distinguish between a goat and a
koala, except for the latter's delicious fragrant fur:
eucalyptus scented. Hunting a koala would have taken
considerably more stealth and luck, mind. Koalas
spend most of their time in trees and dogs don't climb
trees. In order to take a koala, Sophie would need to
have come across one on the ground and have been

hungry and aggressive enough to have seized the hunting moment.

Nervous koalas get from tree to tree by moving carefully from branch to branch. The koalas on St Bees live so free of threats that they're more likely to climb down, stroll along and then climb the next tree. Bill and Sean have tracked koalas, via their GPS collars, that move all over the island, not just from tree to tree but hill to hill, often leaving their parents to go about independently in the world and possibly feeding from many different types of eucalyptus leaves, not just the specific type it has long been thought that koalas are limited to.

'I was concerned,' says Bill about the presence of Sophie. 'The koalas over there don't seem to worry too much when they're on the ground. They are not used to any ground-bound predators, unlike the ones inland, which are up a tree as soon as they see you.'

Alistair had kept his eye out for the dog and had seen it several times dashing across Homestead Bay's muddy flats. It had seemed ragged, elusive and very self-contained, but certainly not threatening. It wasn't until the last weekend in March, though, that Alistair got a good look at the dog, when he was standing with a recently-arrived Bill and the rangers as the dog ran out from the bush at Shark Point and across Homestead Bay. It looked fit, not as skinny as he remembered from the previous brief flashes. It had a very hefty blue coat and looked rather impressive crossing the flats against the sunset.

Bill was on St Bees to collect specimens from as many of the koalas as he could in four days. Knowing that the dog was there, he would be on the look-out for signs of distress. He also knew he should be prepared for possible koala injury or death.

But while Bill and Alistair noticed changes in the wallabies, there was no sign of stress in the koalas. At least not yet. None of the known koalas were missing, none of them turned up dead on the knolls and there was no sign even of any other ravaged animal carcasses.

Still, this dog had now been seen on both islands and was sturdy enough to have been living out there without seeking the company or support of humans for over three months, maybe more. It was wily enough to have survived a swim across the channel and whatever else it had been through in order to get to St Bees and Keswick in the first place. Even if it wasn't killing koalas, over time it could disturb their peace if they became afraid of a ground predator. There really was no other answer but to get the dog off the island.

14

The Rangers Set a Trap

For a month or so, ever since David Berck's phone call alerting them to the presence of the dog, rangers Ross Courtenay, Steve Fisher and Steve Burke had been meeting in the Mackay offices and discussing how to deal with the animal that first Brian on Keswick and then Peter on St Bees had spotted. 'So, we're thinking, what are we going to do with this dog?' recalls Steve Fisher.

Dealing with sick or wild animals was part of their job, and they'd been destroying goats for years. They were professionals and knew that eradicating non-native animals for the sake of the natural flora and fauna on the islands was their duty. This was different, though. This wasn't a feral goat, it was a dog, and all of them were appalled at the idea of having to destroy it. But the problem was that nobody knew how long it had been out there and how wild it might be. If it was feral and vicious, death might be the only option.

'We talked a lot about how to handle the situation, what was for the best. We wondered, do we let the dog starve to death? But, no, we couldn't do that. That's inhumane, we couldn't let a dog starve. Do we shoot it? If it was a wild dog, maybe. But shooting was definitely a last resort,' Fisher explains.

'I was very keen on trying to trap the dog. The logical explanation was that it was somebody's pet,' says Burke. 'That was the only way it would have got there. Which meant that it might not have been too wild, and that we should try to get it back to Mackay.'

'We never once came up with the idea that it had fallen overboard from a boat and swum there, and that people might be still looking for it,' says Fisher. 'That would just never have occurred to us as a possible explanation. We thought, someone's abandoned the dog and that's a pretty cruel thing to do.'

The rangers consulted with the Mackay Council workers who dealt with lost or abandoned domestic animals all the time. They discussed the possibility of trapping the dog, hoping that it was in a friendly enough condition to bring it back to the mainland. While it was a long shot – the dog had showed no intention of being lured by Peter Berck – trapping gave the dog the best chance of survival.

The Mackay Council agreed to loan the QPWS marine park guys a spacious, wire, animal trap for Burke to take out to St Bees on his next trip. He and his colleagues were going out to do some maintenance on the lantana, which had been eating its way across the island, along with prickly pear. Prior to the dog's arrival, these plants and the goats were St Bees' main feral pests and predators. The rangers were only going to be out on the island for four days, though, and Burke knew catching the animal could be tricky.

The rangers talked about what they'd do if they could trap the dog and it was in any state to be domesticated or rehabilitated.

'We actually thought it was a long shot because what dog, especially one that had been out there for a while, is going to walk into a trap?' admits Ross Courtenay. 'But we had to give it a go. And as long as the dog wasn't savage, we planned on taking it back to Mackay. We probably would have put an ad in the newspaper. We just kept coming back to the idea that it had to be some-one's pet.'

If no one came forward, they could take it to the pound for assessment and, hopefully, adoption. 'We would have found a home,' says Ross. 'As a last resort, one of us would have ended up keeping it!'

On the morning of Friday, 27 March, Steve Burke, Ludi Daucik and several ranger colleagues, along with Bill Ellis, arrived at the south end of Egremont Passage and moored their boat, *Tomoya*, just at the edge of Homestead Bay. Sophie was over on Honeymoon Bay when they arrived. She was now three months into life on St Bees, five months into island life altogether.

When Steve Burke first saw her, it was through his binoculars. He was standing on the bow of *Tomoya*, surveying the island to see if he could catch a glimpse of any goats or interesting wildlife activity or flora developments. He scanned north to Shark Point, up through the bushes and rocks that led to hills, zooming in closer as he hit the tree line, spotting a curlew here, the tail of a lace monitor lizard there. As he moved east over Homestead Bay, and then all the way around to the south side of the island, he caught sight of something shiny and white in between two trees, just at the edge of the beach line on Honeymoon Bay. He zoomed in but still wasn't sure – it looked like the skeleton of something, but it was bulbous. It looked like a turtle shell, a rare sight on St Bees as turtles are so stealthy. Burke shifted the binoculars so that he was looking at the beach, and caught a moving grey and blue mass. It was Sophie, rolling around, legs lolling about as she rubbed and rolled her back and her tummy all over the sand.

'She was having a fat old time,' Burke remembers. She looked as though she'd just been swimming. Any onlooker might have imagined that she wanted to be there. For now, Burke was excited just to sight this elusive creature.

Mid morning, the rangers motored into shore on

the tinny to drop off Bill, who was meeting with his volunteers and staying at the south house, and the rangers walked up to Peter's house to say g'day. Peter was not long back from his medical treatment in Brisbane. The rangers had called ahead to tell him that this was the weekend they were going to try to trap the dog. Peter didn't admit it but he was nervous for the animal – while the rangers were telling him that they hoped they could save it, Peter knew that any hint of hostility would end in death. And given that he hadn't been able to bring the dog in himself, he was sceptical. But he wasn't going to interfere with the rangers' job.

Steve Burke told Peter that he'd spotted the dog already through his binoculars, rolling around on Honeymoon Bay. 'Makes sense,' said Peter, who had figured the dog was sleeping either there or one beach along, at Stockyard Bay. 'It's coming closer to the house now,' he told Steve. 'It might have got a whiff of the Pal I'm leaving out. Still doesn't want to get too close, though. It just won't quite show up.'

They discussed where to set the trap, considered Honeymoon Bay, and decided to wait it out and see if the dog appeared anywhere else.

Two nights later, the dog did make an appearance, trotting across the flats of Homestead Bay just as the sun was starting to set, as Bill was looking out to sea with Alistair, Steve and Ludi. It was a Sunday evening.

'There it is,' Burke said to Bill.

'Lone dog in the wild,' Bill replied.
It was time to set the trap.

While Bill and Alistair were watching the sunset and
Steve and Ludi were setting the dog trap, David Berck
and his wife Carolyn were starting to think about dinner
over in the Mackay suburb of Eimeo. David opened the
freezer and realised that the family had plenty for a
barbecue. 'Why don't we get Jodi and Ray over here for
dinner,' he said to Carolyn. It was a spur of the moment
idea but it was the way things rolled over in Eimeo.

Jodi Manning and Ray Cook had been neighbours
with David and Carolyn for years and had spent many
a weekend on St Bees with them and many a Sunday
night in the Bercks' Eimeo backyard feasting on steak,
potato and salads. Jodi and Ray walked right over.
Carolyn opened a bottle of sauvignon blanc and David,
a jovial, heavyset bloke who loved to entertain, got
barbecuing. The four of them started talking about their
weeks while the Bercks' children, Hayley and Tyler,
played with Jodi's two dogs, Rani and Jack.

David had a story. 'So, there's a wild dog on the
island,' he started, turning a steak over as he spoke.

The conversation paused.

'What do you mean?' asked Jodi.

'It's a stray dog that seems to be bringing down goats.
It's been there for months, we've had to call the
authorities.'

'What sort of dog? Where did it come from?' Jodi

asked, ever the dog enthusiast. Jodi had adopted dogs all her life, including Rani, a most unusual looking animal not for the faint of heart – a very short-haired, wrinkle-prone white thing, a shar pei pitbull cross.

Carolyn and David explained that Peter had been seeing the dog, a blue cattle dog, on and off for a few months and that they figured it must have been left behind by yachters who had come over to camp or picnic. But this blue heeler had scared their friend Frank by growling and hissing at him in the generator shed, and now they were concerned that it was feral and dangerous. The QPWS marine park guys had taken a trap out there this weekend and were hoping to catch it once and for all.

The idea of a dog being dumped on an island was appalling to Jodi. 'How could someone have left their dog?' she demanded.

At first, no one had an answer to that one. As at every point in Sophie's tale, the truth, that she had not been abandoned, that she had survived against all odds and was still very much missed, was too preposterous to suggest itself. But then, in a moment of pure serendipity, Jodi's partner Ray, a fellow of few words, remembered something.

'Didn't your mother's friend lose a dog out that way a few months ago?' Ray said.

The party turned to him. *What?*

Jodi thought about it. 'Well, yeah, but that was ages ago.'

Ray shrugged. 'Just thinking. What sort of dog was it?'

Jodi didn't know. She and Ray had heard the story just a few weeks earlier when they were visiting Jodi's mother, Heather. Heather was Jan's old friend and ladies lunch partner, the one she had called, just after Sophie's disappearance, to tell everything. Jodi had assumed the missing dog was a poodle or something similar – a small, manageable dog, just like Heather's Carly, perfect for boat trips. Not like a cattle dog at all.

'All I know is that they're a slightly older couple and they used to take the dog on the boat,' she said. 'They were devastated when they lost it.'

Ray had planted a seed and as the Sunday evening evolved, as glasses were topped up, the conversation escalated about the mystery of this dog surviving out there on St Bees. All of a sudden, there was the possibility that it could be more or less a family friend. Everyone let the story run, laughing and calling out over each other, imagining the long-lost pet being rescued and reunited with the family. They tried to picture who would play the dog in the movie, who would play David, who would play Frank who had thought the hound was a wolf. And all through it, Ray had a niggling feeling.

'I didn't even know what sort of dog Jan had lost, but Ray said, "let's just give it a chance. You never know",' Jodi recalls. 'I guess we were getting all excited about it.'

When Jodi and Ray walked home some time around nine, Ray was still hooked on the possibility of a fairy tale ending. 'Why don't you just ring your mother and find out?' he suggested.

Jodi, still in the spirit of the evening, thought, *Why not?*

It was half an hour later when the phone rang at the Griffiths' and startled Dave, who was sitting watching TV. Jan was already in bed, weary from a weekend of activity. The couple had had a lounge-y evening and Dave was just about to follow her when the phone rang. Dave grumbled to himself – *what time was it?* – but figured it was one of the kids calling. He was in the mood for a bit of a chat, anyway.

In fact, it was Jan's friend Heather.

'G'day Heather,' said Dave, perplexed. He thought this a strange time for Heather to call. 'Jan's gone to bed already.'

'I know I'm calling late,' said Heather. 'But I had to phone you. Look, bear with me, Dave. I've got to ask you – Sophie, she was a cattle dog wasn't she?'

The question jolted Dave. It was Sunday night, he was ready for bed and here was Jan's old friend calling and asking him about Sophie. Dave wasn't used to hearing her name out loud.

'Yes, she was a cattle dog,' answered Dave. 'A blue one, she was blue. What's going on?'

'I knew it!' said Heather. 'Listen, this is going to sound a bit far-fetched but I might have some news.'

As Heather spoke, Dave's heart rate increased. This was a bit of a stretch, and yet . . .

Heather reiterated that if there was any chance it was Sophie, they'd have to start making phone calls first thing in the morning. This dog was going to be trapped any day now – it was all set up.

Dave had a feeling. A positive feeling mixed with dread. He thanked Heather in a bit of a daze, hung up the phone, sat down, and thought, *well, what do I do now?* He was bursting to wake Jan but the stark contrast between a potential miracle and further heartache was already making his head spin – there was no way Jan would sleep a wink if he woke her now.

The house had become disturbingly quiet. *This is a bloody long shot*, he thought. *What are the chances?* But the positive feeling was so strong that he had to tell someone. So he called Bridget.

'There's a dog on St Bees,' Dave blurted out when she picked up.

'What are you talking about?' asked Bridget. She was sitting in her flat in Brisbane chatting with her room-mate, Sammy. She could hear the hopeful excitement in her Dad's ordinarily stoic voice. 'Your mum's friend Heather just called. Her daughter Jodi knows the owner of the island and there's a wild dog out there. We're thinking it might be Sophie.'

Over in Brisbane, Bridget stood up. 'Dad, you're not serious?'

After all these months, now this news? Father and daughter felt a bit light-headed.

'Listen, don't get your hopes up,' warned Dave.

'We're going to call the marine park guys tomorrow. Whatever you do, don't tell any of the others. Let's just wait and see.'

Dave hung up, leaving Bridget dumbfounded and shaking. How could she go to bed now without calling one of her siblings? Ellen, who lived just a few blocks away, was heavily pregnant, tired, and working. She shouldn't disturb her.

But Bridget couldn't keep it in. So she dialled Ellen's number. 'There's a dog on St Bees and it might be Sophie!'

Ellen had been snoozing in front of the TV with Ben and when she saw it was Bridget calling, wondered what her little sister wanted on a Sunday night. This was the last thing she expected. They hadn't spoken about Sophie in months.

'What? Is this even possible?' she said to Bridget.

Both sisters were excited and terrified. *What if it wasn't her? What if it was her? Could she really have swum there? What if it was her but she'd gone feral and she had to be put down? How would Jan and Dave cope? How would Bridget cope?*

Ellen and Bridget made a pact to call each other the minute they knew anything more.

15

. . . *Sounds Like it Could be Your Dog*

The next morning, Monday morning, 30 March, Jan woke at six thirty to find a note from Dave on the kitchen table.

Call Heather. It's about Sophie.

Her first thought was, *Oh my God. What now?* Then she felt an awful ache and put her hand to her heart, as she had on the St Bees beach, months ago. Seeing Sophie's name jarred her. She frowned. Her day was taking on a surreal tinge.

She glanced outside. There was Ruby, her tail whipping madly against the screen door in the hope that this would be the morning that Jan finally invited her inside.

Jan phoned Heather immediately. She didn't beat around the bush. 'What's going on?' she asked her friend. Jan had one hand pressed to her forehead and was starting to sweat a bit. *What was going on, here?*

Heather told Jan that Jodi had been over at her neighbours' the night before and had called afterwards in a somewhat incredulous state. Apparently Jodi's neighbour, David Berck, said there was a cattle dog on St Bees. It all seemed pretty outlandish and coincidental, really, but Jodi's Ray – you know how quiet he is – had a feeling. And now Heather had it, too. When Jodi said the dog had been mistaken for a wolf, Heather knew, *This dog could be Sophie.*

Jan couldn't get her head around a word she was hearing. *How was this possible? Was she dreaming? Sophie? Still alive?*

When Heather told Jan that the rangers were out there that very moment trying to trap the dog, Jan snapped into action. The two women hung up and Jan immediately dialled the number for David Berck that Heather had given her, her hand shaking a little. Jan counted the ring tones, willing someone to pick up the phone. It rang several times, then clicked. Jan breathed in, ready to speak. But it was the answering machine. 'Hello, this is Jan Griffith calling,' Jan said. 'We think the dog on St Bees might be our dog.' She didn't bother with niceties. She was already in a state of shock.

Jan put the phone down and her eyes scanned the living room, distracted. She looked out at Ruby, still waiting for some attention, and put her hands on her hips. *What was she supposed to do now?* If what Heather had said was true and the dog was being trapped and it could be Sophie, then they had to get out there. *But where? Who should they call? And . . . what? Sophie? On St Bees?*

Jan was incredulous, but then she started to think back to that day on the beach. New Year's Eve. That nest she'd found with the animal skeleton. The feeling she'd had. *Could Sophie really have been there? How far from where she went overboard was that? Surely not.*

She called Dave on his mobile.

'Is somebody pulling our leg, Jan?' Dave asked, not really joking. 'It was late when Heather called last night, I thought she was crazy.'

'I couldn't believe your note, this morning,' Jan conceded.

'Let's just see what David Berck says, hey?'

Dave was feeling anxious about investing too much in the possibility that this dog was Sophie when they really had very little information to go on. It was surreal, for sure. 'I mean, she was a good swimmer but . . .' he trailed off.

They made a plan. Dave would call David Berck again and if they didn't hear back from him, they would try the Parks and Wildlife guys. It was still early in the morning but if there was any truth to Heather and Jodi's story, they had to try everything they could.

While Jan sipped a much-needed cup of tea at the

kitchen table and went through the phone book looking for the number for the QPWS Mackay office, Dave tried calling the Bercks. It took a few attempts. The Bercks were in the throes of morning chaos and not expecting a call.

Finally David Berck answered the phone and told Dave that it was Ross Courtenay he needed to call. He also warned Dave not to expect miracles. 'Look mate, I don't like your chances here. As far as we know, she's been bringing down goats and has the thirst for blood. It's going to be up to the authorities to make that call.'

Dave heard it: The call was whether the dog needed to be destroyed or not.

He put the phone down and called Jan. He gave her the number to call Ross Courtenay. He told her what David Berck had said. 'Who knows, darl. It could be her. It's bloody hard to believe but it could be. The thing is, she might be feral. Apparently this dog has been bringing down goats.'

Jan nodded silently on the end of the phone. 'I don't know if I can take this,' she said simply.

Dave was quiet.

Both of them were thinking, *can we go through this again*? They had only just found their footing with Ruby, who had become the tiniest bit mellower in the past few weeks. They had agreed to take her for juvenile dog training together, and now, after her third lesson, it seemed that while she was still a bit of a wild thing, she was learning quickly. They were feeling as though they could be proud cattle dog owners once again. Now here they were, getting their hopes up that despite all the agony of the last five months, this story might really have a happy ending.

The Griffiths went into action mode. There was not much use in talking about the negatives. Or the positives. Both of them felt it. They had hope. It really could be her. It all just seemed right. But the clock was ticking and there was no time to hang around ruminating. According to David Berck, the rangers hoped to be trapping the dog this morning.

'Call this Ross Courtenay guy,' Dave said. 'Call me back and let me know what he says.'

Ross Courtenay took a phone call in the QPWS Mackay office. The lady on the other end said she'd heard that somebody had reported a dog on St Bees. She seemed to think it might be her dog.

Ross was sceptical at first: this dog had been out there for months and today of all days, when the rangers were going in with the trap, this woman, Jan Griffith from Mackay, calls up and wonders if it's her dog.

He wasn't even ordinarily in the office at that time on a Monday morning. 'Jan was lucky she got through to me,' Ross admits. 'It was completely random that I was in the office that morning and if I hadn't been there, there was nobody else who knew anything about the mysterious dog.'

Ross, with his own rescued mutt at home, could hear the desperation in Jan's voice.

'I know it sounds ridiculous,' she was saying, her words falling out in a rush, 'but this dog, who we foolishly lost, is our beloved pet and we have mourned her and felt terribly guilty. We have to give her every chance.'

When Jan told Ross that the dog's name was Sophie – Sophie Tucker – and she was a cattle dog, Ross had the same rush of optimism that David had the night before: it was Sophie. He could feel it.

'It does sound a bit crazy but, well, it sounds like it could be your dog,' Ross said.

Over on *Tomoya*, where the rangers were sleeping, Steve Burke was having his morning coffee when the phone rang.

'Ross was telling me that someone had lost their dog over by Hesket Rock back in October and her name was Sophie or Sophie Tucker,' Steve recalls. 'It was a little surreal – this call was coming through today, after all these months of hearing about the dog and wondering why nobody was claiming it.'

'It's unbelievable, I know,' said Ross to Steve. 'It sounds like her dog, though. It could have swum.'

This timing was incredible but still, it gave Steve hope that maybe they could trap this dog after all. The bafflement all along for the rangers had been why, if someone had lost their dog on the island, they hadn't contacted them?

'I thought it was a bit strange at first. If I lost my dog overboard, the first thing I'd do is contact Parks in case we'd seen it,' Steve admits. 'But then when we found out the circumstances, that they lost her five nautical miles off the coast, we could understand why we didn't hear anything.'

Steve got in the dinghy and zoomed it over to Stockyard Bay. He walked up the shore to the bushes, his boots crunching over the debris of twigs and shells. Behind him the tide was low. Had he not been working, he might have gone for a dip. The clear water was inviting even in less than perfect weather.

Steve crouched down. The angular green leaves of the beach-scrub tree poked at his forehead as he peered into the trap. It looked as though the dog had been there – there were paw prints all around. But it was nowhere to be seen – Steve looked up the shore, across to the line boat on Stockyard, scanning to see if the dog had just left. He hoped he could catch a glimpse of a tail or back legs disappearing across the rocks into the bush. Nothing.

But Steve consoled himself with the thought that the dog was intrigued. It had come close enough to touch the trap with its nose. He peered closer through the gaps in the wire. It hadn't touched the hessian bag, which was now well and truly seeped in gravy and attracting ants and flies. He marvelled at the dog's canniness: it must be hungry. There was food and drink on St Bees, for sure, but they weren't seeing the amount of goat carnage they'd imagined a dog could get into in three months, and there was certainly no evidence of any wallabies or koalas having fallen. *Wasn't it starving? Was it so wild that it didn't need any store-bought Pal? Or was it so smart that it knew that the trap could mean danger?*

Steve made sure that there was still enough beef to lure a dog in. The beef hadn't gone rotten but as the gravy seeped, it was getting more and more pungent. If the dog was already curious enough to have sniffed around the edges of the trap, how long could it really hold out on taking a swipe at the food?

He took a walk up the beach of Honeymoon Bay, remembering seeing the white turtle shell wedged between the casuarina trees when he scanned the area from *Tomoya* a few mornings earlier. He was curious about it. Turtles would come into St Bees to lay eggs in the spring and summer months, exactly the season when Sophie was there. This was a big one, a hundred kilograms or so, but there was nothing left of the turtle but its shell, mostly whole but for a few jagged flints snapped off around its edges. Steve crouched down to take a closer look. The shell was not going to budge. He flinched. This was sad. The turtle must have got trapped there on its way back to the water. He wondered if the dog had discovered it – it would have made a good feed. He saw no paw prints around but it did look as though something had been getting into this turtle. He scanned the beach, seeing windswept ripples in the sand, remnants of crab shells and beach scrub.

There was still no sign of the dog.

Throughout that day, Steve Burke, Ludi and Bill traipsed up and down the hills of St Bees. A few of the rangers were spraying lantana and prickly pear cactus over on Turtle Bay, on the east side of the island overlooking Aspatria, while others helped Bill and his volunteers fulfil his mission of catching and sampling his fifteen koalas in four days. All the while, the men were on subtle alert for the dog.

On Tuesday morning, 31 March, Steve woke again around sunrise, fixed himself a cup of coffee and fussed about *Tomoya*, peering through his binoculars and admiring the early hours. He looked over to the island but could not quite see the trap. The day before, not long after he'd inspected the trap to find paw prints around it, the weather had become gusty and the water in Homestead Bay choppy. The rangers had decided to move *Tomoya* over closer to Keswick Island to avoid the risk of hitting the bottom in Homestead Bay.

They hadn't seen the dog the day before and Peter, who had said he'd make sure to keep an eye on the trap from his house, had not called him with any news. Steve was wondering if this would be a failed mission – the rangers were heading back to Mackay today. If they couldn't catch it this time, they'd have to consider other measures. Nobody wanted that.

At around seven that morning Steve answered his mobile phone. It was Peter. 'You've got it,' he said. 'I can see the dog, it's moving about, probably not very happy, but you've got it, it must have been starving.'

'Are you sure?' Steve asked. He was excited but realistic.

'I was still sceptical – could it suddenly be this easy?' Steve confesses now. 'Maybe Peter had just seen a shadow.'

He and Ludi got in the dinghy and motored back over to Stockyard Bay. The closer they got, the clearer it became that the metal trap was no longer empty. Steve and Ludi could hear the dog barking as the boat drew closer, and they could see it moving, pressing itself up against the cage and sticking its nose through the wire.

As they rode the tinny onto the shore and hopped out, Steve prepared himself for a struggle. But he remembers the dog being gentler than he anticipated.

Sophie was whimpering and pressing her nose right through the cage wire. She was sniffing in and out anxiously, her breaths loud and frantic, and looking directly at the rangers as they approached her. Her hackles were up but her eyes were friendly.

Steve assumed this was the Sophie Tucker that the Mackay woman had called Ross about the day before, and so he and Ludi started to say her name as they approached her. 'I started saying, "How you going Sophie?" '

Sophie barked. She was alert and on guard but her tone was not vicious. And when she heard her name, she tilted her head.

'I think I'd expected some wild dog to be hissing at me, because she'd been there for three months by herself,' says Steve. 'But she wasn't like that.'

Sophie was barking and moving around in the cage, trying to step her paws through the wire. Her head was tilting and every so often she paused, looking Steve square in the eye. Then she'd bark again, as if to say, *I am a dog and I'm scarier than I look.*

Steve didn't buy it. 'It was pretty cool,' he says. 'She kept barking but it wasn't aggressive. It was more of a, *who are you and what do you want?*'

She was looking at him, as if to say, *how do you know my name?*

'I pretty much knew then that it was her, that it was their dog.'

Burke and Ludi, looking at each other incredulously, knew they should move swiftly. They threw a towel over the cage and carried it down to the dinghy. As the tinny powered through the water, Sophie became more anxious. She was barking and moving to and fro in the cage. After all this time alone, facing the elements, she was being hurtled along in a cage, prevented from seeing where she was going. The rangers were taking her to *Tomoya*, moored not a few hundred metres from the airstrip where, in all probability, three months earlier Sophie had waded in on the trail of the scent of survival.

Back on the boat, Steve phoned Ross, who could hear a dog barking in the background. 'We've caught the dog! We're heading back to Mackay now.'

'You're kidding,' Ross said. It wasn't even nine o'clock and they'd already caught the mysterious dog and found the owners. He and his colleagues were somehow becoming involved in a Hollywood story.

'She was in there this morning, Pete called to tell me. I didn't believe it myself but we've got her and she seems OK. She looks a bit skinny but she's not threatening me,' said Steve.

Sophie had been throwing herself against the cage, wanting out, but when they got her onto *Tomoya* and were talking to her, saying, 'Good girl, Sophie,' she started to settle. She even sat down in the cage, though her ears were still alert and her hackles up. That tail was not yet wagging.

Meanwhile, Bill Ellis, who was waiting on *Tomoya* to get a ride back into Mackay, wasn't feeling so optimistic. Bill has a different memory of Sophie's temperament on the way back into Mackay and was nervous riding on the boat with this wild animal that had looked so independent and cinematic running across the shoreline at sunset just a few days earlier.

'The dog was quite upset about the whole proceeding,' Bill remembers. 'It was snarling.' Bill figured it was a good idea to try to calm the dog as much as possible. He tipped a bottle of water upside down to drip it into her mouth. She took a few licks but wasn't going for it. She was either not thirsty or she was too suspicious (or angry) to hydrate.

'She did calm down as we neared the marina,' Bill

remembers. 'I think she knew where she was. But I was telling myself, *be careful where you put your fingers, you're gonna lose one.*'

As Bill got off the boat to stand on the marina deck where he could see the action but easily escape it, Steve and Ludi stood next to the cage. Steve took his camera out. Ross had probably called this dog's potential owners right now. It wouldn't take them long to get here, and he wanted to capture the moment. Everyone, by this time, had a feeling: they were about to witness a miraculous reunion. The animal was no stranger to people. It might be scared, and they weren't about to pat it, but its bravado was fiercer than its intention. This dog was somebody's pet and it appeared to know its name – Sophie.

16

Hey Tuck, Where've You Been? – the Reunion

It was Tuesday morning, 31 March. Monday had passed in a bit of a blur. After the morning's ring around, Jan and Dave had gone about their day as usual but neither could concentrate. They went to Oscar's and they went to the office. Jan stopped by the butcher on her way home and took Ruby for a walk and that night, over dinner, they chatted, their attention wandering to Ruby as she grunted and gazed at them through the screen door, wagging her tail at any hint that they might throw her a scrap. Neither of them wanted to talk about Sophie. It was feeling like a repeat of all those months earlier when they had driven through the gate with no Sophie in the backseat, unable to speak her name. Only this time, there was hope in the air. This time, the energy was positive. Jan could have popped it with a fingernail.

On the Tuesday morning, having slept surprisingly well, Jan bumbled around getting dressed. She was on autopilot. She knew that if Ross didn't call today, he wasn't going to call. This was the final day that the rangers were on the island.

She was spraying some perfume when the phone rang. It was Ross Courtenay.

'G'day,' Jan said.

'They've trapped the dog,' Ross said. 'They're on their way back to the harbour now and you are welcome to come down and meet them. The dog is pretty tense but we've got her.'

'Right,' said Jan. She wanted to say, '*Is it her?*' And then, if he said, '*I think so,*' she would have said, '*Are you sure it's her? Are you sure?*' But her throat was closed over.

'Oh my God,' was all she actually managed. She wanted to cry. It was now that the possibility that this might actually be Sophie really hit her. Or that it might not be her – it might be someone else's beautiful blue cattle dog. *If it was her, what had she been through? Would she remember them? If she was feral, would she be aggressive towards them? Could they handle seeing her like that? Could they handle seeing her feral and then having to have her put down?* It was suddenly all too much.

'Look, if it's her, she's apparently looking remarkably healthy,' said Ross, as if sensing the rush in Jan's mind. 'The rangers are telling me that they're not worried about her. She was in the trap this morning and they picked her up not long ago. She's a bit upset but she's OK.'

Jan hung up the phone, swept her hand through her fringe and immediately called Dave at work. She couldn't waste a second.

'You ready?' she said. Jan was trying to hold it together. *One foot in front of the other* was running over and over in her mind.

Dave made it home in record time. As he drove through the gate, his hands were gripping the steering wheel and his heart was thudding.

Jan came out to meet him. She looked the perfect picture of a boating woman on a mission: she was wearing a striped shirt and had her sunhat in her hands.

Dave's brow was furrowed as he got out of the car to greet her. He walked towards her and rubbed her back as she put her cheek out for a kiss. Jan looked up at Dave and they locked eyes.

'We're going to be all right,' Jan said.

'Yeah. Yep,' said Dave. 'Yeah, of course. We've just got to give her this chance.'

'I have a good feeling. I know I shouldn't say it, but I do.'

Ruby was out there with them, her doggy radar telling her something was up. She jumped on them as they walked back to the car and Dave didn't even yell at her. All he said was, 'You stay here, Ruby. We might be going to get your sister.'

Dave grabbed Sophie's lead on his way out of the carport, and gave Jan a look. *Just in case.* They could hardly bring themselves to believe the best-case scenario, but they were brimming with optimism. Dave put the lead in his pocket.

The anticipation was overwhelming and there had been no time to prepare for whatever it was they were in for. *Were they really on their way to pick up Sophie?* The Griffiths knew they could be headed for grave disappointment. They knew their hopes were too high. *When had something like this ever happened? She was a dog. She'd been gone for five months. They'd circled for hours looking for her on that terrible day. How could it be that, all this time later, here she was?*

The couple were beside themselves on the drive down to the marina and spoke no words. Jan was clutching the passenger door handle with her left hand. Dave seemed to take every stop, every roundabout in slow motion. The radio was tuned to the local ABC news radio station but neither of them heard it. Dave parked in the marina car park and Jan's door was open before the ignition had turned off. They gave each other a sideways glance and Jan raised her eyebrows as Dave swiped the key and, upon hearing the beep of access, started to walk down the ramp. They could see *Tomoya* and the rangers in their khaki shirts milling about.

The cage didn't become visible until they had almost reached the boat, at which point they saw a thick coat of blue fur moving about inside a large cage.

'Oh my God, Dave,' Jan yelled, grabbing Dave's fore-arm, 'it's her!'

'Sophie!' Jan called. She already knew.

'Tuck, hey Tuck!' Dave called out. The blue fur stopped banging about and began to wiggle and whim-per and throw itself against the cage.

Dave and Jan rushed forward. The rangers were all watching in amazement. They saw the dog switch, its mouth transition from defensive growl to glee. Sophie thrust herself at the door, beating and banging the cage against the floor.

Jan was crying. As Dave took long steps towards the cage he called out, 'Hey Tuck, hey girl, where you been? Where you been?'

There was no doubt in anyone's mind: this was the Griffiths' dog.

'Oh my God,' Jan was saying, her hands to her mouth, just as they'd been all those years back when Sophie was a nervy puppy in the pet store. Jan and Dave knew her as instantly as Sophie knew them. That wiggle of her whole behind, like a baby who has just discovered the joys of walking. *This was their girl.*

Dave looked at Jan, and Jan looked back at Dave, both of them only now daring to believe it was all true. 'It's her, isn't it?' Dave said. His eyes glistened. Jan could only nod and smile and brush tears from her eyes. Sophie was alive and she knew them. She hadn't drowned and she hadn't forgotten them.

Bill's concern that someone was going to lose a limb

had subsided. This lone dog was now more like a new puppy. She wasn't going to bite a soul. Jan had turned to the rangers to affirm, it's her. It's our Sophie.

'Seems as though we've found our owners,' Steve said, looking at Jan, who was so choked up she couldn't speak except to say, 'Sophie Tucker! Sweetheart! What happened to you?'

And with that, Steve opened the cage and Sophie leapt out. She bounded for the couple and leapt into Dave's outstretched arms. Dave stumbled backwards. Jan sobbed. If this scene had been in a Hollywood movie there would have been a stirring orchestra and an audience reaching for tissues. Burke and Ludi, burly, rugged rangers that they are, choked up. 'I wouldn't say tears, but our eyes were definitely watery,' admits Steve. 'Mate, it was great. It was an awesome feeling, actually.'

'There's our girl,' Dave said. He was frowning and smiling and looking at Jan and the rangers and rubbing Sophie's chest and cheeks, all at the same time. He grabbed Sophie's front paws and pulled her face to his and said, 'Tuck, what on earth?'

Jan looked at Steve. 'You can't believe how much we've missed this girl,' she said.

'I bet. I do believe it,' said Steve. 'I can't believe how long ago you lost her!'

Jan pushed a tissue to her mouth and the corner of her eyes. Turning to the rangers, she said, 'I can't believe it, I just can't. What did you guys do? How did you get her?'

Steve had first his camera out and then his video camera, determined to capture this incredible moment. He looked up at Jan, grinning, and said, 'canned food! Guess she was hungry, hey?'

He went back to filming, but Sophie wasn't about to prolong the proceedings.

'I didn't get to pat her that day,' says Steve. 'She wanted to get out of there, which is fair enough. I'd want to get away as soon as I could, too.'

Sophie was wiggling and pouncing and barking and once she was off the boat, and Dave had managed to put the lead on her – no small feat, as this recently wild animal had never liked donning a lead even in her most domesticated times – she was off up the ramp, pulling Dave along with her. She was running towards where she knew home was and Dave couldn't hold her. For a minute there, he worried that she might run off, so desperate she was to get going.

Come ON . . . Let's get out of here, Sophie seemed to be saying.

'I didn't even have time to thank the guys,' says Dave.

As Sophie dragged Dave up the ramp, Jan was caught between running along behind them and thanking the rangers profusely over her shoulder. She was mostly speechless. Her mind was spinning with the suddenness of it all. She was in a state of disbelief but she was also experiencing an odd sense that no time had passed since that gorgeous day five months ago that had turned so horribly wrong. Here they were back at the marina that she had avoided for months, and her Sophie was back and seemingly as jovial as ever. She looked up at Dave and Sophie, then back at the rangers, waved her hand, yelled, 'Thank you!'

'Take good care,' Steve told her, still with his camera out and full of adrenaline as he watched this miracle dog heave her owner up the ramp.

Jan saw that Dave was struggling to keep a hold of the lead.

'I thought, *the last thing we need now is that she take off without us*,' Dave laughs.

But even in her haste, Sophie looked behind to make sure that Jan was there too. Then she sniffed her way to the car she hadn't ridden in for five months. By the time Jan got there, Dave was in the driver's seat and Sophie was standing in the back, her head between the seats, looking at Jan, as if to say, *are we going home now?* Her tail was wagging, her tongue was out, and she looked about her, nonchalant as ever. As they drove out of the marina and stopped at the first set of traffic lights, Sophie poked her head into the front seat and licked Jan on the cheek.

Bridget had barely slept the past two nights since her dad had called her, unable to keep the news of Heather's phone call to himself. She and Ellen were both on tenterhooks. Jan was going to be calling one of them soon, there was no doubt.

Bridget was at home waiting for the call.

At work, Ellen was spinning around in her office chair, distracted. She'd told some of her co-workers what was going on and every few minutes someone called out, 'Have you heard anything yet, Ellen?'

Ellen knew her phone was going to ring at any moment with wonderful or terrible news.

Jan started making calls before they'd even got out of the marina. She knew Bridget would be most desperate to know and Jan was desperate to blurt it out to everyone. 'It's her, it's her, it's her,' is all Bridget remembers Jan saying, through sobs. Bridget started sobbing too – child sobbing with snorts and snot and everything. Jan was talking at a rapid pace, how she'd called Heather and then Dave Berck, and how Ross Courtenay had said, 'It's your dog; I'm telling you, it's her,' and how Sophie's coat was thick and furry like a wolf's and how she was 'dragging your father up the ramp at this very minute' and as far as they could tell, she was not feral at all but her old, gorgeous self.

'Call me as soon as anything else happens,' Bridget said, between gasps. Then began a frenzy of phone calls. Bridget hung up the phone to call Ellen. But Ellen's phone was busy. So she called Matthew who was at work and was in a state of disbelief. Matthew then heard from Jan and then the eldest Griffith dialled Luke, knowing full well that he would probably be out of range. Luke was in Indonesia, surfing in Lombok, oblivious to the miracle happening back home. Bridget kept trying to dial Ellen who, she didn't realise, was trying to dial

Bridget. All the while, Jan was trying Ellen, whose phone was busy, so she dialled Luke in Indonesia and she left countless messages to call home: 'There's some news!' Then she called her friend Heather, who started crying, and Heather called Jodi, who was at work and started crying, and when Jodi told all her work mates that the dog she was telling them about yesterday morning, the one on the island that the rangers were trapping, was indeed her mother's friend's dog who went missing months ago, all Jodi's work mates started crying.

Jan got through to Ellen thinking that Ellen didn't know anything yet – when in fact Bridget had called Ellen on Sunday night.

'Finally there it was, a phone call from Mum, and she said something like, "we have some news",' remembers Ellen. Jan started from the beginning, going into the details, as was her way. 'She launches into the long-winded "Janny" version of the story, which she thought I was hearing for the first time.' All Ellen wanted and needed to know, though, was – was it Sophie and was she all right? 'It was killing me. I couldn't pretend for even a second that I didn't know and quickly interrupted her and just said, "Is it her?"'

'Jan said, "Yes! It's her! She's in the car with us now and we're on our way to the vet." '

Ellen hung up the phone, stood up in her chair and said, 'It's her!' All her nearby colleagues cheered and Ellen cried again.

Then Bridget finally got through to Ellen and the

sisters wailed on the phone together. Meanwhile, Ellen's mobile was ringing. It was the koala scientist Bill Ellis. As Bill had been getting off the *Tomoya* at the marina, certain that things were going to go badly, he had been stunned to see that 'the lady' who thought she owned the dog was Jan Griffith, the mother of his great old basketball friend, Ellen. It had been ten years since he'd seen Jan and Dave, but once he'd realised it was them, his fear that the event was going to go badly disappeared. Now he was ringing Ellen to tell her how he'd just witnessed the rescue of her dog, Sophie, from St Bees. They laughed. It was about as small-town a coincidence as it could be.

When Sophie entered her vet's office not an hour after leaping into Jan's arms and dragging Dave up the marina ramp into the car, Dr Katie Nash said, 'Sophie hasn't been castaway. She's been on an island holiday.'

Sophie licked and wagged, lapping up the attention as the girls on the front desk patted and exclaimed over her. She gave herself up freely for poking and prodding and torch shining. She seemed jubilant, wiggling and panting as Jan and Dave patted her and looked on. Dr Nash ran her hands over Sophie's thick coat of fur and plunged her fingers into her neck, checking glands under her legs. Jan and Dave were a bit giddy themselves and just praying that the happy dog they were seeing was for real, that Dr Nash was not going to turn around and deliver them bad news. Sophie's coat was the splendid outdoor coat of a wild animal but it was oddly odour-free – where was the stench from all those nights outside and all those dead things she must have lain and rolled on? The vet and the Griffiths surmised that she must have been swimming – her fur was sparkling. She let Dr Nash inspect behind her ears and take her temperature and she looked at everyone with an open, tongue-wagging mouth as they marvelled over how long it had been since that nightmarish day when Jan and Dave thought they'd lost her forever.

The notes from that visit on 31 March, 2009, show that Sophie was in immaculate condition. 'Bright, alert, responsive,' Dr Nash wrote. 'Good body condition, friendly and excitable.' All of Sophie's physical tests were in normal range, and after a full examination, Sophie was given a clean bill of health. Sophie's current vet, Dr Rowan Pert, came in to visit this dog who, he had just heard, had been living out on St Bees alone for five months. 'I remember seeing a very normal, happy dog and I was just amazed,' he says. 'It was fascinating, as though nothing had happened.'

There was, however, the possibility still looming that while Sophie seemed all joy now, there could be deep-seated physical and emotional issues still to surface. Dave Griffith had David Berck's words in his head: 'I don't like your chances. If she has the taste for blood, it may not be possible to rehabilitate her.'

Dr Nash wrote up a plan for Jan and Dave to follow in anticipation of the very real problems that might emerge. Sophie might develop separation anxiety, just like a child separated from its mother, which meant that she would probably be clingier than usual. She should be fed separately from the other dog; rewarded for her calm behaviour; given plenty of attention and plenty of things to do; not left alone.

As it turned out, all the concern about Sophie's mental state, her ability to return to domesticity and to lose whatever wild, ruthless behaviour she might have picked up on the island, was seemingly for nothing.

Jan and Dave drove their girl home from the vet's, Jan answering and making calls and just loving the sound of Sophie panting happily in the back seat. She turned around to stroke her girl, her head reeling with the reality of what was happening.

As Dave drove the Nissan through the gate, Sophie's enthusiasm rose. They opened the car door and Sophie raced upstairs. She hadn't forgotten the house or the air conditioning. She was sniffing madly, her behind sashaying with enthusiasm as she sniffed around for that old squeaky pork chop. And where were the tennis balls? Finally, the rug, air conditioning, tennis balls!

But as if her ordeal hadn't been enough, there was also a rude shock awaiting Sophie. An addition: Ruby Red.

'She got home and must have thought, *after all I've been through, now you want me to be nice to this red thing?*' laughs Dave, who is utterly charmed by Sophie's handling of Ruby.

As Dave drove through the gate, Jan got out and ushered Ruby behind the gate that separated the pool from the carport, to give Sophie her bearings before introducing the two dogs. Ruby, of course, was a frenzy of energy, running and practically skidding on her claws towards Sophie, ready for a game the instant she laid eyes on her new big sister. As Dave opened the gate, Ruby bounded through it and Sophie froze. Her tail did not offer up a wag. She stood in the carport, legs slightly widened, hackles up. Her armour was in place while Ruby sniffed her, tail mad with movement, and hoping desperately for a tumble. Sophie growled. Ruby went on sniffing. Sophie wasn't threatening to bite. She was letting Ruby know that she better know her place now. As Ruby sniffed her all over, the top dog turned around to look Ruby square in the eye. Ruby was oblivious to the possibility that Sophie might not be so excited to see her. Sophie looked at Jan and Dave with those big, accepting eyes but they knew what she was saying: *Who is this? And how long is it going to be here?*

Jan and Dave walked Sophie around the garden, got the red water bowl out of the storage closet where it'd been all these months, and did a lot of standing and watching their girl in awe.

'How about it, hey darl?' Dave said, watching Sophie and addressing Jan. 'Is she a hero or what?'

'I know this sounds crazy David, but . . . I knew it, I just knew it,' Jan said. She was still thinking about the day on St Bees. But she couldn't go there or she'd *really* start thinking: *maybe they could have rescued her earlier.* But Sophie was home and she was lovely and she seemed absolutely happy.

Sophie sniffed and explored, rolled on the grass and nudged at a tennis ball for a throw. She was showing no signs of anxiety yet. When Jan went to the kitchen to make a few tuna sandwiches for lunch, Sophie was there, sitting in front of the kitchen island, hoping for any scrap of food to fall, which of course it did, because Jan and Dave were so ready to give their girl whatever she wanted. Ruby stayed outside, almost beside herself with anticipation. Sophie pretty much ignored her, sitting with Jan, rolling about on the Turkish rug as Dave and Jan sat at the table and just watched her. Sophie then took her post in front of the table and dropped her legs, landing as if on a pillow on her right side in the stream of the air-conditioner. Jan burst out laughing.

'How long have you been waiting for that, Sophie Tucker?' she said as Dave's eyes seemed to water a bit.

That afternoon it was time for their weekly juvenile doggy training with Ruby. Dave and Jan piled both Sophie and Ruby into the car. Ordinarily they'd have left Sophie at home, but they didn't want to leave her ever again – and they were following vet's orders to include her in all family activities for a while. The class was always a hoot, and Jan loved watching the dynamics play out between the puppies, some of them docile and obedient but most of them, including Ruby, running amok in their own unique ways.

The dogs were being handed treats every time they performed some menial duty, such as walking around the circle or sitting. Sophie wasn't involved, she was just on the sidelines. She started whimpering and barked a few times. 'I couldn't say if she wanted to participate or just wanted a treat,' says Jan.

They eventually had to remove her as she was disrupting the energy, and Dave went and sat near the car with her, chatting and looking at her intently. *Was this the beginning of anxiety?* He was still trying to work out what the hell his girl had been through. He couldn't imagine how far she'd swum, let alone what she'd done all those nights out there on the islands alone. 'Where have you been, Tuck?' he said to her over and over again, as she looked at him and swayed her behind. It was a bit spooky. *What if she did become a nervous wreck, how would they cope with her? She seemed so normal but how could that be?* But all these thoughts were secondary for Dave, who was on a high from Sophie's return. Nothing could bring him down.

Around seven that evening the four of them drove through the gates back home, *at last.* Jan and Dave figured the dogs would be weary from all the activity and Sophie might be ready for her first night back on her armchair.

Jan settled on a lounger at the pool while Dave took a Corona out of the bottom fridge and headed up the stairs. Sophie followed him, wildly excited. In the kitchen, she watched him go for the fruit bowl on top of the microwave, cut a lemon into slices and then head back downstairs to wind down in the balmy evening. Sophie was following him on the tip of her nails. 'Come on, Tuck,' he said. He pulled up one of the deck chairs but quickly noticed that Sophie hadn't joined them around the pool.

'Sophie,' he called.

Jan leaned forward and looked round next to her.

'Sophie Tucker,' Jan coaxed.

She wasn't coming to their calls, so Jan went looking. She found Sophie sitting by her lead, which was hanging in its usual spot in the carport – Dave had put it back there after they'd driven in that morning. Now their miraculous rescued dog was waiting at the gate, ready to go for a run in the paddock just as she had done every day before she went missing.

'It was amazing,' says Jan. 'She knew exactly where her lead was and what she wanted.'

'You want to go for a run, sweetheart? Is that what you want?' Jan cooed.

'Do you remember this?' Dave asked, holding the lead in front of her nose. Sophie began wagging her tail madly, looking at Dave and then at the gate. She was back to her old routine as if no time had passed. Once out of the driveway, Sophie broke into a run, sniffing and bounding her way around the next-door paddock, looking back to be sure that Dave was there and watching her. She brought him a stick every now and again or came and sat beside him to catch her breath.

Ruby followed Sophie, racing circles around her, as if to say, *I'm here, I'm here! What do you want to do now?* as Sophie continued on her explorations of the block of land that she knew and loved so well, especially with the whole bunch of new smells that had arisen, five months after her last jaunt here.

Later that night down in Brisbane, Bridget went over to Ellen and Ben's place with a bottle of red wine. While a very pregnant Ellen sipped soda water, Bridget and Ben had a drink and the three of them video-called Mackay. Dave had just returned with Sophie and Ruby and Jan had given the two dogs three Schmackos each, a tradition reinstated in Sophie's honour.

As the Griffith sisters appeared on the computer screen, Sophie looked at it and wagged her tail, of course completely unsure about where all those familiar voices were coming from. Bridget, putting her face to the camera, called to Sophie, 'Hi baby girl, hi baby girl, you're back!' Sophie looked at Jan and at the computer screen, wagged her tail, looked over at her armchair as if to work out her best option. Then she trotted the few steps from the kitchen table to the Turkish rug and laid down.

Ellen asked Jan how Sophie's first day back had been and Jan vigorously recounted that it was as if she had never left.

'It's just incredible, Nell,' Jan said. 'She's her old self, instantly. It's like, whatever she was doing out there, she hasn't forgotten anything. We got her home and she raced up the stairs, sniffed around the kitchen, wagging her tail. She's been following us around from the second we got home. This afternoon, your dad and I sat on the couch – we're exhausted – and Sophie just flopped in front of the air conditioner.'

Ellen and Bridget looked at each other and Bridget said, 'She's such a star.'

'It's pretty crazy,' said Ellen. 'All this time . . .'

'But when we got home from doggy training tonight – this is the most amazing thing – your dad started chopping up a lemon for his Corona, you know how he does. Well, we called her and called her and she didn't come. She'd raced straight to her lead and she knew exactly where it was. She wanted a run in the paddock next door.'

All the Griffiths were in shock, but the ease with which Sophie had adapted to her first day home made everything seem so positively normal. All the guilt, all the worry, all the mourning and moving on seemed somehow rinsed away, at least for now, by Sophie's presence and her obvious eagerness to be there, by her love for Jan and Dave and the love she received in return.

Bridget and Jan sipped red wine from their respective lounge rooms and Sophie occasionally looked over from her napping spot with happy bafflement. She'd get up and come and sit on Jan or Dave's foot, then wander off intermittently for a sniff around the kitchen linoleum and a lie down under the couch, then come back to the dining table where the action was, to wonder where exactly these sisters of hers were – she could hear them but they weren't there.

The Griffiths blithely welcomed their beloved family member in just the way they would have had one of the siblings been travelling overseas for months and months, catching Sophie up on family matters that had taken place while she was away. 'See Ellen's big belly, Sophie? You're going to have a niece or a nephew,' Bridget said, pulling Ellen's shirt up and rubbing her sister's bursting pregnant tummy. The family began singing to her belly and Bridget told the baby about the family it was about to be born into and how much they already loved it and look! – what a clever pet they all had.

Sophie's ears perked and fell. She looked at the computer and away, plonked herself against Jan's leg and Jan scratched her between the eyes with her fingernails.

Then Sophie, perhaps a little bored, moved over to her armchair, climbed up and flopped down, head propped on the wooden arm for a rest. Her eyes drooped and she looked up and over once more at the family. Then she dropped her head and her eyes fluttered closed.

17

Sophie Goes Domestic
and the Story Goes Viral

In the days and weeks after Sophie returned, Jan and Dave watched her for signs of anxiety. Jan came home a little earlier than her usual lunch or afternoon hour, and Sophie, followed by Ruby, was there waiting for her to pull into the carport so that Sophie could stick her head in the car door. She didn't seem nervous or unhappy, she seemed content and eager simply to greet Jan and follow her upstairs for air conditioning time. When they were at home, they kept Sophie with them and mostly separate from Ruby. Ruby was still an outside dog at that point and spent a lot of those first weeks gazing through the screen door, standing up and wagging her tail every time someone moved, thinking, *this is it, this is when I get to go inside.*

That moment didn't come for a while, though, and for the most part, Sophie didn't seem to pay much attention to this new red dog staring in at her except to express a little bewilderment. When they took Sophie and Ruby in the car to Ruby's doggy traning, Sophie looked at Jan and Dave from her spot on the backseat as Ruby jumped around and was yelled at by Dave, 'Ruby, geddown!' *What's her problem?* Sophie seemed to be asking. Sometimes she'd growl at Ruby when it seemed the red dog was simply too much in her face. There was no aggression, though, and no clinginess beyond her normal affection for the Griffiths.

Finally, the whole family was back together and Dave and Jan, after all those months of guilt and grief and trying to push the horror and the unknowing into the back of their minds, started to feel a little relief. Sophie's presence made them realise how sad and tense they had still been, despite Ruby's adding much distraction and a lot of funny moments to their days. Sophie was both a reminder of how terrible things could get but also of how wonderful their life really was. They felt terribly lucky, almost too lucky, to have her back.

That Sophie returned while Ellen was on the brink of giving birth to the first Griffith grandchild, added to the sense of family bonding. 'It was just a really nice time,' says Bridget. Everyone was in touch, even more than usual, all four kids calling around to update each other. In Brisbane, Bridget spent a lot of time at Ellen and Ben's and then the three of them would go over to

Matty and Melissa's and they would video conference to Mackay and catch up with Jan and Dave, sometimes several times a week. Jan and Dave would be wondering how Ellen's belly was growing and Bridget and Ellen would be wondering how Sophie was fitting back in.

And, just as in Ellen's case, the answer was that Sophie was doing amazingly well. So far, she wasn't showing any signs of what the vet had warned them about. There were a few things that were different: she seemed snappier around meat, for example. She was less gentle when Dave put his hand down with a piece of beef fat. She was still a remarkably polite eater for a dog, though. When Sophie would eat, she'd do it slowly. She wouldn't growl and grunt or inhale a bowlful in one go as some dogs did. She'd take breaks, sometimes taking a piece of meat or fish out of the bowl to break it up into neat pieces and eat them up, one at a well-chewed time. She could lick a bowl clean for twenty minutes, delicately tending to every bit so that it was clean and undamaged. But in the weeks after Sophie returned from St Bees, she had become more aggressive. While Ruby, in some of her rare moments of total obedience, would sniff at a sausage or a bone, keeping her teeth out of it ever so respectful of the giver's hand, Sophie was inclined to snap at the last minute when being hand-fed. She'd sniff the meat out and look at the giver as if to say, *thanks*, but the last second would be an urgent, almost ruthless grab, leaving slobber and prompting Dave or Jan to snatch their hand back in reflex. 'She certainly learnt how to make the most of a kill out there, as now she never wants to give up on a bone,' says Jan.

Jan and Dave spent a lot of time watching Sophie sleep smooshed up against the pool fence outside in the sun, or laying belly-flopped on the wooden floorboards in front of the air conditioner in the living room. Sophie went back to her old routine of nudging her way into their bedroom every morning and waking Dave with a gentle look or a lick, and Dave was more than happy to get out of his warm bed no matter what the hour.

He was also more enthusiastic about the afternoon walk routine. Sometimes he would take the two dogs on his own, or Jan would go with him, Dave taking Sophie, who – after five months of free-roaming island life – would pull a little harder on the lead than she did in her early days and was too strong for Jan to handle on her own. Then, without fail, every day as Dave went for a Corona from the bottom fridge, Sophie and Ruby would get frenzied, Ruby jumping all over him provoking a 'geddown!' from Dave, while Sophie sashayed all over the place but never leapt or whimpered. Then Dave would usher the dogs back through the front gate and they'd run upstairs to where Jan had prepared their afternoon treats: three chewy beef Schmackos each, lined up like toast soldiers on the kitchen bench. Sophie's three Schmackos would be lined up on the left, and Ruby's on the right. Jan would hand them one each at the same time, as the two dogs sat, Sophie with her legs splayed like a kangaroo, looking up at Jan with wide eyes. Unlike meat, both dogs would receive their Schmackos gently, chewing them up and looking to Jan to hand them the next one until all six treats were gone.

No sooner had Jan and Dave begun to feel as though life might really be back to normal, when the world got involved. The week after Sophie arrived home, her story ran on the local ABC radio station and appeared on Channel 10 and in local newspapers across the country. The day after the story ran on the ABC, Jan and Dave walked into Oscar's for their usual breakfast routine. Desley was there and John was working the coffee machine. That day, he personally brought the skinny latte over to Jan, put it down in front of her and said, 'How did I not know about your dog? How did you keep this to yourselves for months?'

This time, Jan and Dave were not so shy about the facts. 'We got our Sophie back,' Jan announced proudly. And the questions began: 'What happened to her and how was she?' 'What was she, some sort of super dog?'

'God, I remember that horrible day that you told me about her getting lost. I felt so terrible for you,' Desley said.

'We didn't tell many people, Desley. We were so ashamed,' Jan admitted.

Jan and Dave didn't really know, of course, what had happened to Sophie. There were a lot of questions they couldn't answer, questions they would like to have been able to answer for themselves. *How did she*

*survive? How far did she swim? How did they suddenly
have her back?*

'It's hard to believe, isn't it?' Desley said, almost
speechless. 'What a wonderful story. I'm just so happy
for you. What a girl.'

Jan and Dave told John and Desley, Jenko and other
friends around town, who called the Griffiths' home
after seeing Jan and Sophie on the news, about the
incredible coincidence of Jodi's connection to the
Bercks and the last-minute barbecue over in Eimeo. Jan
was especially thrilled by Jodi Manning's partner, Ray
Cook, who remembered the story of the friend of Jodi's
mother whose dog went overboard, and his insistence
on following it through, *just in case* it was this woman's
– *her* – dog.

Denise and Ian Thomason called Jan, having heard
the news, and Denise had a flashback to that night out
at Scawfell. 'I *knew* there was something wrong that
night,' Denise said. 'I can't believe you've been going
through this. What a story.'

'We'll never pass by St Bees without thinking of
Sophie again,' said Ian.

The attention didn't stop at home. Sophie's story hit
Europe before the week was out. The news of the heroic
dog's island survival and her seamless, blissful, almost
unbelievable reunion with the Griffiths had the world's
attention within days.

Dave's older sister, Janet Khan, and her husband,
Peter, were sitting in their living room in Haifa, Israel,

where they had been living for 27 years, watching the BBC news. On came a news story from tropical Queensland. Janet was curious – this was where her brother Dave lived. The story honed in: it was set in Mackay, which was Dave's hometown. Janet sat forward. Her sister-in-law, Jan, was on TV. That was Dave's dog, smiling from the family pool area, taking Schmackos from Jan's hand. 'There were Jan and Sophie in my living room.' Janet started calling all her friends, most of whom were already watching the news. 'It felt as though half of Israel were watching. We were so excited.'

Ellen dined out on the story for months and it became a friendly game between her friends: where will Jan and Sophie be spotted next? The pair were on every channel and in gossip mags. Luke even had friends in China and the UK who called him when they saw the news.

Over the coming days and weeks, everywhere they went, the story of Sophie would come up. Both Jan and Dave told of how amazing the rangers had been in allowing them to come and see the dog and in not ridiculing Jan for believing that her pet might have performed such a feat. Jan told people that even the rangers had been baffled by Sophie's survival against all the odds.

'It's amazing that she managed it,' Ross Courtenay says. 'There wouldn't have been much meat left on any goat carcasses from culls but I suppose the hides and a lot of bones could have kept her going.'

Jan and Dave are fairly certain that Sophie found a

way to dine on the Bees goats. When they watch her now, attacking and demolishing whole bones, they figure she had to have been feeding on something. In the past, a bone could last her days. In the first week after her return from the island, they watched her at a barbecue, sucking on the marrow of chop bones and crunching each one like it was a bug. They fretted that she was going to choke. But Sophie licked her lips clean and hoovered over the ground for chips that might have spilt from her mouth. She looked up at them, hungry for more. It made Jan think back to New Year's Day on St Bees when she'd found the nest of goat bones on the beach. *Could she really have been that close to Sophie, that day?*

'It just makes me sick to my stomach to think that I didn't call out to her. I was thinking that she could have survived. Why didn't I call out?' she says now.

But all those pangs of regret paled in the glow of the high they were on from the moment they knew it *was* Sophie in that cage on *Tomoya*. Jan and Dave walked around town with effortless smiles on their faces for weeks. They held hands walking into Oscar's and leaned in for a kiss more often than usual. They were being woken once again every morning by the clack of Sophie's toenails on their bedroom floor. Jan's first sensation was, once again, the wet of Sophie's tongue as she leapt over her to follow Dave outside. They now regarded Sophie's tugs on the lead as they walked her and Ruby, (or any resistance to being asked to move from in front of the air conditioner) as nothing but a source of pride and relief.

'I believe that she calculated everything she did,' says Jan, figuring that Sophie's inherent stubbornness at home paid off on the island.

Luke agrees. His theory is that Sophie stopped on at least one, possibly two islands before she got to Keswick, where she was first spotted by Mike Barnett and then Brian. 'She would have dragged herself up onto Aspatria, waited there until she got herself together and assessed the situation. Just as we would have done,' he says. *Hang on, there's a rock, it's exposed, I don't have to swim. Bang. I need to rest. Survival.* Aspatria was an achievable resting point before taking off to St Bees, where she could smell food.

But when people asked about the day she went overboard, Jan and Dave choked up. They were able to give the basics – they had hit the Hesket Rock channel, they left her on the main deck for several minutes, somehow she fell in, they circled around and around for her and they were frantic that they couldn't see her after so little time. And they realised that she couldn't have survived, that she must have hit her head and drowned. They were so ashamed and so full of grief that they could barely tell anyone, even their own children.

The constant going over of the details exacerbated the very mixed feelings the Griffiths had about all this attention. On the one hand, Jan was thrilled. She was so proud of Sophie and felt so blessed to have been reunited with her that she wanted to sing it all over town. But it was also a bit perturbing. Suddenly, images of their family pool area were being cast all over the world and one of the most terrible days of their lives was being broadcast at cocktail hour in places as far as Japan and Israel and the UK.

The story was, of course, being dramatised: Sophie was a miracle dog who had survived on an abandoned, tropical island and had been eating baby goats for five months. Sophie's ordeal was morphing very quickly from a family story, one for the Griffiths themselves to digest, celebrate and recover from over time, into one of those buzzy, water-cooler stories verging on urban myth.

Jan and Dave weren't the only ones swept up in the media craze. Not long after Sophie returned, David and Carolyn Berck flew to Macau, where Carolyn's brother lives, and where the story of this incredible swimming dog was all over the news. The airline staff on Carolyn and Dave's flights brought it up as soon as they heard where the Bercks were from. Indeed, the Bercks not only knew the story, they knew – and leased – the island on which the dog had survived for three of its five months in the wild.

The story made it over to Ashington in the UK, a small mining town outside of Newcastle, and home to the parents of Ray Cook, Jodi Manning's partner, without whose excellent memory and insistence on following his instinct, Sophie might have been sent to the pound.

Ray's parents woke up one day to a photo in their local paper of this smiling, sparkling blue dog who had swum through shark-infested waters, survived on baby goats and – a worrisome glitch in the reporting – koalas.

The increasingly fact-challenged story was that this iconic Australian dog, who had survived in the iconic Australian region of the Whitsundays, had kept herself alive feeding on the flesh of the iconic Australian marsupial, the koala. Somewhere along the line, after local ABC radio reporter, Kim Kleidon, had investigated the story and run a feature interviewing Jan and Dave, David Berck, Brian Kinderman and Steve Fisher, the fact of there being koalas on St Bees morphed into the story that there were koalas on St Bees and Sophie had been killing and eating them.

Steve Fisher was quoted in a Queensland newspaper as having said so, and the news went viral. It wasn't true. It prompted comments ranging from 'disappointed' to 'disgusted' on newspaper sites. People were outraged that this dog had supposedly survived at the expense of koalas. It also called into question the handling of the dog by the QPWS Mackay office, whose charge is first and foremost the natural flora and fauna of the area's national parks.

There were other overhyped reports running in papers and on blogs all over the country, some of them including distortions of facts such as how long Sophie had been left unattended on the boat. These prompted some very negative responses from readers, comments such as, 'someone call the RSPCA,' and claims that Jan and Dave were irresponsible pet owners.

Bridget was less than happy about all the attention – good and bad. 'I just thought, if people could see Dad every night, barbecuing the dogs their own steaks, or the way he looks at them. It's ridiculous how much Mum and Dad love their dogs. . . . In the end, though, I was just happy to have my dog back,' she says.

Dave and Jan felt the same way. The media stories were surreal, but at the same time, both of them had to keep reminding themselves that actually, the core of the story was very real indeed. Their Sophie was back. They had lost her in one of the most isolated, tropical parts of the world and she had survived. What was there not to be proud of?

18

Nobody Else's Girl

'We're just so flattered,' Jan told journalists who asked her what she thought had brought Sophie back to them. 'Apparently, she was never going to be anybody else's dog but ours.'

The Griffiths will never really know how Sophie survived out there, but they're all in awe of how she held out so long, waiting for them. 'I didn't think she had it in her,' Luke admits.

'You can't go against Mother Nature, she'll beat you every time. It just wasn't time for Sophie to go,' says Warren.

Jenko concurs. He was reeling when Jan called to tell him the story, just after Sophie got home. 'I wouldn't have put money on her making it to land. She was fairly sooky for a cattle dog. She was quieter and friendlier than they usually are, not reserved or shy but laidback. Placid. I was really surprised. I guess all her breed's instincts kicked in. And she kept her mouth shut!'

What was it that made her stay loyal to the Griffiths for so many long, lonely months?

Sophie's vet, Dr Pert, continues to be astonished by several elements of Sophie's story. He can't believe she swam so far and he can't believe that she chose to swim again, several months into her ordeal. Most of all, he's confounded that she didn't give herself up for some human love and companionship. 'Why she didn't mooch in for a meal or for a bit of friendship is what I can't understand,' he says. 'She's such a normal, domesticated dog.'

Sophie's breed was definitely an advantage. 'A cattle dog was the best friend I ever had,' says Dr Pert, whose first and most endearing dog was a blue heeler that went with him everywhere in his university days. 'Their loyalty is more intense than in some breeds. Some dogs are pack animals, interaction between everything around them is very important. Cattle dogs tend not to have that. They are far more focused on one bond, with the owner. Other dogs are more aware of the pecking order.'

Pert's dog was his first real buddy, he says. It's a sentiment frequently expressed by cattle dog owners and devotees, like Jenko, who filled Luke's head nearly two decades ago with how unparalleled a pet Jordy would be. 'If you have their trust, there are no dramas,' Jenko says. 'They are just really sturdy, intelligent and strong-willed dogs and I know what it's like to lose one that matters.'

Jan's experience with her childhood cattle dog, Biddy was part of the reason the Griffiths were such cattle dog fans in the first place. 'They are so intensely loyal, sometimes it makes you cry,' she says, having experienced the breed's magic long before Sophie pulled off her astonishing feat. Biddy would follow Jan's baby sister around, gently nudging her if she ever strayed into the next-door neighbour's property. Jan also remembers that Biddy was wary of men, running circles around the girls whenever a guy attempted to walk into the yard. 'You just cannot believe how much they love you.'

Like most dogs, Sophie was not shy of expressing her displeasure at being separated from the Griffiths. Jan and Dave had witnessed this in her even before her time away. It was one of the reasons they took her on *Honey May* initially – they couldn't stand to disappoint her. The pup always knew – and objected – when someone was going away, be it for a cappuccino down at Oscar's or a week in Vietnam, where Jan, Dave and Bridget recently travelled.

For at least a day beforehand, as Jan and Dave finalised details, packed suitcases, and arranged for Luke to move in to dog-sit, Sophie sulked around the house and garden, not trotting out of her spot as she usually did to say hello when she heard Jan or Dave coming her way. When the day came for the Griffiths to drive to the airport, Sophie lay inside the driveway, head between her paws, looking around but not lifting her nose from the ground and definitely not approaching her owners for pats and licks as she did when she was happy. When Dave drove the car out of the driveway, Sophie stared towards the front gate, tail down and motionless. Jan could barely look. *Had she behaved like this on the island?*

On the one hand, Jan and Dave feel a little flattered to imagine that their Sophie was prepared to hang out for as long as she had to, for just one more day with them. But if they'd known this while she was gone, it would have torn them up to think of her suffering alone and missing out on the essential affection that she lapped up when at home.

'I still feel so emotional about her arrival on the island. Imagine how tired, thirsty and hungry . . .' says Jan, trailing off. 'I can see her just lying on the sand with her head on her paws, looking sad and exhausted.'

How, then, did she survive all that time without them when in the past, a few hours or a day felt like too much? The Griffiths wonder, *day after foodless day, night after shelterless night, did she ever curse them? Did she feel even an inkling of rejection? Was she aware of how much time was passing and did she lose faith in the hope of a reunion? Were her memories of Jan and Dave starting to grow fuzzy as time wore on? Was her attachment to them ever threatened? And why didn't she seek solace with some of the other humans she encountered?*

For over five months, Sophie chose loneliness and hunger rather than contact with humans she didn't know and love. She could have relished her newfound freedom, spending her days on the island with Peter as her best friend. It was an opportunity to become a beloved pet but still enjoy the wild that dogs are physically built to revel in. She could have woken every morning to a sunrise over her private ocean bay, spent her days chasing yellow-crested cockatoos and spangled drongos, rolling in mud and sand and chewing on coconut shells.

She did none of this – all the accounts of Keswick and St Bees residents and visitors point to Sophie remaining skittish, suspicious and solitary for five months. In the three or so months it's presumed Sophie was on Keswick, no bins were ravaged, no laundry room nooks or outdoor sheds inhabited. Keswick residents heard barks in the night, sighted paw prints around the beaches and the island tracks, but for the majority of her time, Sophie remained elusive if not downright antisocial. 'Even native animals like skinks and monitor lizards have been known to come inside houses. But not Sophie,' says Keswick's Eva Browne-Paterson.

Dogs are loyal. And cattle dogs are known to be *really* loyal, but the Griffiths believe even their other cattle dogs would have befriended people on the islands, not being able to cope without company. Sophie didn't seem to have this problem.

'I just reckon her sole purpose was to get somewhere where Mum and Dad could pick her up,' Luke says, adding that his dog, Sonny, 'would have waited six hours, then gone, *sod this, he's not coming to get me, what's up? Oh good, there's someone to pat me and scratch me.*'

'Ruby would have been the same,' says Jan, imagining

the red dog all grins and panting at the first promise of love. Not Sophie. 'I believe she got to St Bees and when there were people on Keswick, she swam over to see if it was us. I think this, romantically, but she is certainly resourceful enough.'

'It surprises me that she never went to anyone. You'd think there would have come a stage when she would,' says Ian.

While breed determines a lot in a dog's nature, it does not dictate everything about the way a dog conducts itself. Nature and upbringing work together. There was a stark difference between the personalities and attitudes of Sophie and her predecessor, Jordy. Jan wonders whether this has more to do with nurture than nature, Jordy having been raised primarily by Luke, who would rile her up, wrestling her, chasing her, roughing her around. For Luke, this was because it was a ton of fun but also because he had a traditional, Cesar Millan-like approach to raising cattle dogs. 'The Australian cattle dog is a working breed that requires a demanding physical and psychological regimen,' writes Cesar on his blog, Cesar's Way. 'If left unfulfilled, cattle dogs become easily frustrated.' Luke, who now tries to take his two-year-old and hyperactive blue heeler, Sonny, everywhere he goes, is all about a dog as physical playmate.

'Jordy regarded us as her job – she was guarding us all the time. When we got home, she'd run around the edge of the garden before she came to greet us on the steps,' explains Jan. 'Sophie, the minute we come through the gate, she's jumping onto our laps in the car, she's just so excited that we're home. I think Sophie must have decided that she was just meant to love us. Perhaps, because Bridget was so lavish with love and affection, she got used to it.'

Sophie's instant switch back to playful, adoring dog the moment she heard the Griffiths' voices on the marina five months after going overboard, suggests a simplicity to Sophie's love and loyalty. She just never forgot that it was her job to love and be loved by her family.

Two weeks after Sophie's return, Bridget came home for the Easter holidays. As she flew into town to be picked up by Jan at the airport, she was a little nervous. She was going to see Sophie for the first time in months and she was worried. *What if she doesn't remember me? What if she's mad at me?* Bridget fretted. 'I wanted to say to her, it wasn't me that lost you, baby girl. It was them. Please don't hate me,' she says, only half-joking.

As Bridget drove through the gates to the house, she readied herself for whatever treatment she might be in for from the dog who'd been through so much. But as the gate opened, there was Sophie, bounding towards the car to her original bestie, her behind moving from side to side, mouth open, tongue lolling, smiling in her dog way. Bridget opened the car door and cried, 'Hello, baby girl!' Sophie jumped straight in, landing her whole wiggling self into Bridget's lap and looking at her straight in the eye. Bridget wrapped her arms around her Sophie, brought Sophie's head up to meet hers and ruffled her around the neck. Bridget was tearing up and planting big kisses all over Sophie's neck.

Ruby, still outside, tried to get in on the action, lifting a paw up into the car, attempting to nudge herself up between Sophie's nose and Bridget's. Neither Bridget nor Sophie was having it, though. The girls were back together and they needed some serious alone time. This was Sophie's moment – yet another one – and Ruby was going to have to deal with it.

'She slept in my bed for the first night just like she used to,' says Bridget proudly. The slumber party didn't last long, though. Jan and Dave allowed one night on the bed, then it was back to the armchair for Sophie. Tough. They wanted to instill *a little* Griffith family discipline back into their heroine pet.

Sophie, respectful as always, complied. In fact, despite Bridget's brags that she always gets Sophie on her bed the first night she's back, she has to admit that it may be more Sophie, than anyone else, insisting on the order. When Bridget says goodnight on her subsequent nights home, Sophie is usually already in her armchair, and rarely makes a move for the hallway door leading to Bridget's room. She'll whip her tail on the wooden arm of the chair, lapping up all the goodnight snuggling and cooing that Bridget is giving. She'll happily be picked up and lugged around by Bridget throughout the evening. But Sophie has her armchair and she seems perfectly content with her place in the house.

'She looks at Bridget as if to say, *you had your one night. I'm a dog, I have to do my dog thing,*' explains Jan, the stern authority who Dave had to convince to allow Sophie in the house all those years ago. She is charmed once again by Sophie's doggy dignity. 'They're dogs, we respect that. Just as our kids have their own lives, we respect that.'

Sophie has certainly resumed her role as top dog with quiet gusto, slotting back into the Griffith household as fifth child. In fact, she could even be accused of being a little more haughty than in her pre-island days.

It's somewhat sacrilegious to pick a favourite from the dogs at the Griffiths', but throughout Sophie's first year back when Ellen and Ben came to Mackay with Molly, the first Griffith grandchild, Ruby threatened to nudge her older sister off her perch. Sophie just didn't seem very interested in the baby. Ruby, on the other hand, found a best friend in Molly, who would squeal in delight when she saw 'the girls' and would dangle her little hand down from her highchair to have it licked by a careful and adoring Ruby. Last Christmastime, when Ellen let the dogs in for breakfast while the rest of the house was sleeping off holiday joviality, Ruby was rewarded when she was allowed to share Vegemite toast and yoghurt with Molly in the kitchen, while Sophie darted straight past the action to stand at the door to Jan and Dave's room.

Sophie seems to be not only primarily devoted to Jan and Dave but also quite miffed at being more frequently asked to stay outside when Molly is around. When the baby stands at the screen door calling out to 'the girls', giving herself a dirty nose from having her face pressed against the screen, Ruby will stand nose to nose with her, oozing affection. Sophie will often sit on the next step down, looking up at Molly with heavy eyelids and barely a wag of the tail.

The top dog is generally more prone to sulking since she's got home from the island. Luke has become especially impatient with it, having had to deal with Sophie's moods when he's come to housesit when Jan and Dave have gone away. 'She will go into their room and not come out for days,' he says.

Luke brings the manic Sonny over to the house to live there with him and Heather. While Ruby makes efforts to play and interact, Sophie has none of it. While she's gentle and friendly with Heather, it would seem she has decided that Luke is the reason that Jan and Dave are not there, and she has been known to sulk for up to three days. It gets to the point where Luke will have to take food into the room for her. Otherwise, she'll lay under the leather couch in the living room, only her tail or her nose poking out from under it.

'She gets so annoyed that Dad's not there. And I bring Sonny, so her little bubble has disintegrated. She gets that sulking from Bridget,' Luke laughs.

After a few days, though, Sophie warms up. Perhaps she has been listening to the activity out in the house, to

Heather and Luke talking and playing with the other dogs, the TV murmuring in the background. It's usually when Luke opens a packet of chips or wriggles a packet of Schmackos that Sophie will saunter out of Jan and Dave's bedroom, having returned to her contented self.

None of this can dampen Jan and Dave's pride. Sophie has earned herself something of a pass in the way that wise old women can be forgiven for a little grumpiness at times.

'Sophie has done all the dog things she needs to do for a lifetime,' Jenko reckons. And Jan and Dave might sheepishly agree. Nowadays, there is no question of Sophie's place on the Griffith family tree. There is no question of whether she is allowed inside, whether she's allowed to lick the dinner plates clean, whether she should be sleeping in on her leather armchair, day or night.

Life is pretty sweet since Sophie got home. Jan and Dave are no longer empty nesters, they have two adorable dogs living with them and providing plenty of entertainment. Every afternoon around four, the energy level starts to rise around the house as Sophie and Ruby gather themselves from whatever they've been doing. Their body clock is telling them it's that time: walk time. If they're at the screen door because they've been asked to go outside for a while, Ruby hovers with the tip of her nose touching the screen, as Sophie stands alongside her looking down the stairs, feigning that she's not nearly as concerned as her silly sister. If it's teeming with rain, Dave does his best to ignore them, as he can't look them in the eye and then not take them out. Most days, as Jan puts her sneakers on, Ruby leaps in circles and bounds under their feet as they come down the stairs, in anticipation of that gate opening; not for someone to leave them but for the girls to head out into the world. The four Griffiths take off down the road. If Jan takes Sophie, she spends most of her time winding the lead tighter around her hand to try to keep her within walking distance. Just like old times.

'Cesar Millan says you must be in control of your dog,' she says. 'I don't think I've quite got that down.'

Later, at dinnertime all the family are present: Jan and Dave and 'the girls'. As Jan and Dave sit down to eat, both dogs sit to attention, backs to each other like the hands of a clock: Ruby looking up at one food-bearing owner, Sophie at the other.

Who is going to drop their plate first?

As Jan and Dave negotiate their plates of food, a stack of crispy potato edges and bones (with sneaky bits of meat left on them) begins to pile up on the side of each of their plates. Often Jan can't resist and drops both her hands down to feel Ruby gently remove a chunk of *coq au vin* from one hand and Sophie snap a chicken piece from the other.

Sophie and Ruby have several insider routines and despite Sophie's frequent weariness at Ruby's frivolity, as time passes, Sophie seems to become more attached to her sister. When Dave or Jan drive through the gate, they'll see Ruby run out to the backyard and come back with Sophie trailing behind her. *They're home!* the red dog seems to have informed the blue dog. Dave often comes down the stairs in an afternoon to find the girls wrestling. Ruby will bound over to where Sophie is lying comfortably curled, and nudge her head into Sophie's neck. The two will roll over and interlock forelegs. Sophie bares her teeth and locks her jaw around Ruby's, then proceeds to lick and snarl at the same time. All the while, the thud of Ruby's tail on the ground continues as Ruby bulldozes her head or her nose further into Sophie.

While Ruby still plays second fiddle to her older sister, she has also benefitted from the ways Sophie continues to carve out domestic bliss. When Sophie first returned from the islands, Ruby was still a boisterous pup and Sophie, flopped on the rug inside, couldn't help going in to bat for her. Sophie would every now and again raise her head and look out at Ruby. Sometimes this seemed to be a tease, but over time Sophie would occasionally go to the door and touch her nose to the screen and look back at Jan or Dave as if to say, *we should probably let her in too, no*? It didn't take long for Jan and Dave to cave and these days Ruby enjoys most of Sophie's privileges.

When it comes to bedtime, each dog takes their respective armchair, Ruby on the left, Sophie on the right. Ruby still sometimes tries her luck at getting the sofa instead of the armchair for the night. She also loves to play the game of 'sleep on Sophie's chair', a trick that earns her endless reprimands from Jan, and especially from Dave. She will slide off the armchair and onto the couch, then off the couch as she looks at Dave, opening his mouth to yell again, and finally climb onto her own armchair. Sometimes, Dave will walk into the living room to find Sophie standing at the foot of her armchair looking up at Ruby, who is sitting on it, wagging her tail. Sophie's tail will be laid out behind her, somewhere between a wag and a threat, as if to say, *you've got ten seconds, no more.*

Sophie, of course, gets what is rightfully hers and none of it seems to deter either Ruby or Dave, who will happily play the game with both dogs every night. Dave is even more of a softie than he was before Sophie went overboard. In Sophie's lifetime, he's gone from disciplinary stickler to mush. From a man who believed that a dog's place was out in the yard, to a man who will patter out of bed when he can't get to sleep and stand in the doorway just gazing at Sophie as she snores and croons, always thrilled that she's being watched by the man she is most loyal to.

'There's my girl, hey?' Dave will say, leaning in the kitchen doorframe in his boxer shorts, one bare foot propped on top of another. He'll cross his arms and rub his shoulders, all the while looking at Sophie as she sleeps. She might lift her head and stretch it around to look back at Dave. The end of her tail will move and, as he comes over to her, she'll lick her lips in anticipation of the affection she knows she's in for. Dave will pat her softly between the eyes or rub her behind the ears with both hands as she grunts from the back of her throat and the tip of her tongue moves in and out in appreciation.

Sophie isn't a normal dog. She's achieved a totally unprecedented feat, one that Dave and Jan never expected to be a part of. She has exhibited freakish endurance and loyalty to levels that no amount of dog science could have prepared them for. And she's become a bit of a star because of it. The whirlwind of TV, newspapers and magazines worldwide, a film in the offing and even this book, all celebrating this astonishing, yet seemingly ordinary, family dog.

To this day, there is a framed photo of her in the Mackay rangers' office, Jan's handwriting scribbled across it announcing, 'I've gone domestic!' Nowhere is she more a star, though, than in her own home, where she's living (as the magazine articles said when she returned from the islands) a dog's life.

'They're dogs, they don't ask for much compared with what they give in return,' says Dave these days. 'So we should just give them what they want.'

The Griffiths will never know what Sophie went through out there, the exact details of her extraordinary journey. They wish they could ask her sometimes. But when she looks up at them with those trusting eyes and that soft, blinking gaze, they think they know one thing: that the loyalty and love between owners and dog, and the bond that always felt just that bit more special with Sophie than with other dogs, somehow brought about a miracle.

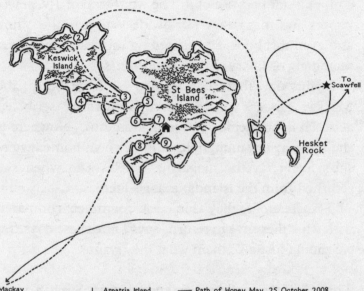

SOPHIE'S JOURNEY

From 25 October 2008 to 31 March 2009
(based on reasonable assumptions and sightings)

Keswick Island

St Bees Island

To Scawfell

Hesket Rock

To Mackay

1. Aspatria Island
2. Connie Bay *
3. Keswick airstrip *
4. Arthur Bay *
5. Vincent Bay
6. Shark Point *
7. Homestead Bay *
8. Honeymoon Bay *
9. Stockyard Bay *

—— Path of Honey May, 25 October 2008
---- Sophie's assumed path through the islands

★ Sophie goes overboard, 25 October 2008
✛ Jan discovers a nest
⌂ Peter Berck's House
✕ Sophie's trapped, 31 March 2009

* Areas where Sophie or her paw prints were sighted

Acknowledgments

This book belongs to so many people and quite a lot of places:

The Griffiths. For so many reasons, their love for Sophie above all. My life will never be the same with you all in it. I do believe you were a family born to be written about.

I could stop there, but I won't.

To my Mum, a dog lover if ever there was one who thought it would be nice for me to come home for a while to write. Regret it, much? Love you Mum. To Rob, also whose internet connection I deeply offended throughout and whose red wine supplies I not so sneakily depleted. And to Ionela Cornhill to who I can now say, 'Yes, I've finished the book yet!'

To Dad and Sue whose 'Never Give Up' emails with that overused picture of the pelican and the frog actually do work on me. Thanks Dad. To Lisa and Martin, who continue to (attempt to) make a Fair Lady out of me.

To Erin Hosier, who all but dropped this whole enterprise into my lap and whose 'take heart' got me through many early days of uncertainty and then final days of editing (and uncertainty).

To my editors – and there were several. To Lisa Highton and Renee Sedliar, first and foremost, who believed first in Sophie and this book and got it – and me – over the finishing line. To Deonie Fiford and Helen Coyle who taught me so much, both with such a light touch. My future writing owes itself to you two, I do believe. And to Valerie Appleby, working behind the scenes and no doubt a future queen of publishing.

To John and Lauren at Oscar's Café, for me a little piece of Brooklyn in Mackay.

To all the dogs in my life especially, though Molly, Chloe, Lucy, Molly (another one), and Oscar, who were there throughout the duration of writing and provided much inspiration, never failing to make me laugh spontaneously out loud, coo, wonder deeply and talk like a fool.

To Briana and James at Shots of Happy for being naughtily awesome as well as interested and for making the best soy latte in Forster, NSW.

To Byron Bay.

To a handful of great, enduring friends in my life who I hope know who they are and so don't need to be named.

To Steve and Oscar: best dog-to-Dad dog bond ever.

To the Mackay based rangers at Queensland Marine Parks and Wildlife who cared about the mysterious blue dog way beyond their call of duty. To Andrea Dobbyn, a patient and efficient go-between for this pesky, constantly on-deadline journalist and the rangers who were just going about their lives.

To Peter Berck, who I wish I could have known better. To St Bees island.

To Bill Ellis, Sean Fitzgibbon and Jason Wimmer, who taught me what little I know about fuzzy grey bums and corrupted me while I was supposed to be working. Bill, I'll beat you in dice, yet.

To the residents of Keswick Island for living where they do and caring about the elusive blue dog. Especially to Brian and Lyn Kinderman and Jero Andrews, without whom Sophie's story would be an even bigger mystery.

To Ruby, who is one heartstoppingly good-looking and infectious dog.

Most of all, to Sophie, the most dignified dog anyone is likely to encounter.

Picture Acknowledgments

Most of the photographs are from the Griffith family collection. Additional sources: Corbis/photo Matthieu Paley p11 below. Hodder & Stoughton/photo Daryl Wright p1, p15 below, p16. Brian and Lyn Kinderman/ Keswick Island Guest House p7, p8 below. Koala Research Centre of Central Queensland p11 centre right. Emma Pearse p6, p9, p10, p12 above. Queensland Department of Environment and Resource Management (DERM)/photo Steve Burke p12 below. Rex Features/ photo Daryl Wright p13 centre and below. Jason Wimmer p11 above right. Daryl Wright p8 above.

photograph © Steve Trudgeon

EMMA PEARSE is an Australian journalist who lived in New York for over ten years, where she wrote for *New York*, *Slate*, *Salon* and *Village Voice*, among others. Emma now lives and works between Australia and New York. *Sophie* is her first book.

Further Reading

Sophie's journey is one triumphant example of the loyalty and physical endurance that dogs can exhibit. In researching Sophie's story, I was assisted by many wonderful works of research, analysis and anecdote by behaviourists, scientists, trainers, dog owners and authors far more expert on the life and mind of dogs than myself. Below is a list of books, far from exhaustive, that can help any dog lover understand their domestic animals.

Emma Pearse

Animals in Translation: The Woman Who Thinks Like a Cow by Temple Grandin and Catherine Johnson (Bloomsbury, 2006).

Animals Make Us Human: Creating the Best Life for Animals by Temple Grandin and Catherine Johnson (Houghton Mifflin Harcourt, 2010).

The Dog Who Couldn't Stop Loving: How Dogs Have

Captured Our Hearts for Thousands of Years by Jeffrey Moussaieff Masson (HarperCollins, 2011).

When Elephants Weep: The Emotional Lives of Animals by Jeffrey Moussaieff Masson and Susan McCarthy (Vintage, 1996).

The Emotional Lives of Animals: A Leading Scientist Explores Animal Joy, Sorrow, and Empathy – and Why They Matter by Marc Bekoff (New World Library, 2008).

Dogs That Know When Their Owners Are Coming Home: And Other Unexplained Powers of Animals by Rupert Sheldrake (Arrow, 2011).

Australian Cattle Dogs by Richard G. Beauchamp (Barron's Educational Series Inc., U.S., 2008).

For further information on the places and fauna Sophie's journey brought her in touch with, visit the following links.

Keswick Island: www.keswickisland.com.au

Queensland Department of Environment and Resource Management: www.derm.qld.gov.au

South Cumberland Islands National Park (Department of Environment and Resource Management): http://www.derm.qld.gov.au/parks/south-cumberland-islands/

Australian Koala Foundation: www.savethekoala.com

Australian Cattle Dog Society of NSW: www.acdsocietynsw.com

Koala Research Centre of Central Queensland: www.cem.cqu.edu.au/FCWViewer/view.do?page=9218

The bond between animals and people . . .

We very much hope you've enjoyed the amazing story of Sophie and her adventures. At Hodder we love animal stories and like to think we publish some of the best.

Please visit our website and have a look at what we do. You'll find some of the most loved stories and some perhaps you're not yet familiar with. *Marley & Me*, *Dewey*, *Cleo* and *The Puppy Diaries*. We also publish the Dog Whisperer himself, Cesar Millan.

If you want to leave a comment on Sophie or any other books or sign up for our newsletter, we'd love that too.

www.hodder.co.uk